CW00351505

TASTY **STORIES**

LEGENDARY FOOD BRANDS
AND THEIR TYPEFACES

For Mil – *see the beauty in the everyday things of life*

TASTY STORIES

LEGENDARY FOOD BRANDS
AND THEIR TYPEFACES

Joke Gossé

LUSTER

FOREWORD
BY TOM ANDRIES

Love Letters

I fell in love with beautiful packaging and typography at a young age.
My Aunt Laura had a little grocery shop in the centre of town. The store-
front was a beauty: a central wooden door with rounded glass windows
on either side. Inside there were mosaic floors and wooden furniture with
white high ceilings and art deco lighting. People came in to buy cigarettes,
food, drinks… or simply to have a chat with Laura. Children bought the
candy displayed in big glass bowls on the counter, sold in homemade paper
bags. Laura didn't have a calculator; she did the counting on a piece of
paper, and every price tag was handwritten. The shop smelled of freshly
ground coffee and tobacco.

To reach the top shelves you needed a ladder. Those shelves were filled
with printed cans, beautifully illustrated boards and enamel signs. I fell
in love with the beautiful women displayed on these boards, the illustrated
pictures with great typography. The classic packaging designs in matching
colours: iconic brands like Coca-Cola, Belga, Ca-va-seul, Côte-d'Or,
St-Michel, Spa, Hero, Kwatta, Cécémel, Stimerol, King, Liebig,… I couldn't
stop staring at this colourful design world on the top shelves in Laura's shop.

So it should not come as a surprise that after secondary art school I studied
advertising and graphic design. My huge interest in type design prompted
me to take typography lessons with Luk Mestdagh. In my last year I designed and digitalised five typefaces; Luk was my mentor.

My first job was for a packaging design agency in Brussels that, except for me, only had English designers. We designed packaging for Belgian brands such as Kwatta, Belga, Bockor and Anco. I fell in love again, this time with English design and packaging – and started to get to know all the London-based agencies, like Pentagram, Landor, Pearlfisher, Coley Porter Bell... Packaging was for me the perfect combination of type, image and idea – all in one. I consider good packaging like a true piece of art.

Even when I'm on holiday, I love to go to shops and discover local brands and products. I only buy packaging for the design. I remember a trip to France where I found a beautiful enamel Casino sign designed by Cassandre at an antique market. It was far too expensive, but I had to have it. So I ended up borrowing the full amount from friends.

My passion became my profession. I'm fortunate to make a living by designing or redesigning brands. At our agency Today we aim to match strategy logic with design. We want to create iconic brands and timeless packaging based on a client's true story. As designer I respect the history of these brands and try to translate their story into contemporary design.

I still miss Laura and her shop, but luckily I can find comfort in the iconic brands in this lovely book by Joke. I love the craftsmanship in her work and her books. It is an honour to write a few words in this book and to enjoy the stories and the great design.

Tom Andries
Brand Designer
Creative partner Today, Belgium

PREFACE
BY THE AUTHOR

I have loved typography for as long as I can remember. My fascination with typographic shapes started when I was still in school, developing into a true passion as I studied graphic design in college and entered the world of typography with its rules and extensive terminology. The beauty of the black shapes contrasting with the white paper, the combination of straight stems with elegant curves and well-formed terminals and serifs... they got me every time. I also discovered how type can convey a message through it shapes and style. How a word that is typeset in bold condensed sans serif type tells a completely different story than that same word set in a light curly connected script with a swash capital. Letterforms can be a powerful means of communication, adding an extra dimension to the content of a text.

During my education as a type designer at the University of Reading in the UK, I learned a lot about the history of type and typography. All type styles are historically rooted; they were developed alongside the great art movements and reflect the style of their time. Typefaces can be described not only as seriffed, condensed, economic or elegant, they can also be classified as belonging to a Renaissance, classicist or post-modern style.

I find it immensely interesting and fascinating that historic type styles are not outdated, even though production and printing techniques have changed enormously since the first metal printing type at the end of the 15th century. Even typefaces that are used today are either digital versions of typefaces that were designed years or centuries ago, or they are at the very least inspired by historic characteristics.

For example, the typeface in which this text is typeset (Lyon, designed by Kai Bernau), is inspired by the work of the 16th century punchcutter Robert Granjon, and yet it is still perfectly suitable for contemporary use.

As a type designer, paying close attention to letterforms has become second nature to me – both in my work and in my everyday life. When I'm reading a text or a word, I'm constantly going back and forth between understanding what it says and analysing the shape of the letters. What strikes me every time is that the details are so much more than mere details. Smaller features like serifs, the shape of curves, contrast etc. define the type style and the message being expressed.

In this book, the history of 23 legendary food brands is directly linked to the different type styles that have been used in their advertisements and packaging throughout the years. Some brands have at certain moments in time chosen to change the typestyles in their logos and packaging rather drastically, others have done so by making very subtle changes in style. Recognising these changes sometimes requires paying close attention to details in the different letters. This is one of the things this book would like to achieve: the texts take their readers by the hand and help them look at letters and images closely, by describing, sometimes in detail, what's there to be seen. It's a great way to see the products we use every day in a different light and, by extension, to look at the world from a new perspective. Most of the brands included in this book can be found in household cupboards the world over. The lettering and logotypes define the look of the brand and are an intriguing gateway to discover the history and the stories behind them. I hope you enjoy reading this book as much as I did researching it.

Joke Gossé

CONTENTS

CHIQUITA

SINCE 1870

14

Chiquita was founded by Captain Lorenzo Dow Baker in 1870. The company was originally an American railway venture, but started planting bananas on the grounds bordering their railway tracks in Costa Rica. Eventually the export of fruit turned out to be more worthwhile than the transport of people. The company expanded and Chiquita became the most famous banana brand in the world, and remains so today.

A great deal of the company's branding success has to do with its mascot logo: Miss Chiquita. She was created in 1944 by cartoonist Dik Browne (known for his *Hägar the Horrible* comic strip) and first appeared as an animated banana, wearing a flamenco-style dress and a fruit basket as a hat. [1] [2] In that same year the jingle *I'm Chiquita banana and I've come to say* hit the airwaves, with vocalist Patti Clayton singing the original voice of Miss Chiquita. At the peak of its popularity the jingle was aired 376 times a day on the radio. It is also one of the few spot commercials that still lives on today.

Having embodied the company's brand identity for such a long time, Miss Chiquita is undeniably one of the most notorious brand personalities in history and an important element of the logo. Early on, in the 1940s and 1950s, hardly any attention was paid to the type in the logo, not even for the brand name. [3] The type in this example must have been added to the illustration at a later date because it is typeset in Helvetica, a typeface that was only released in 1957.

In 1963 Chiquita had a large and significant branding campaign. One of the novelties introduced at that time was the now famous blue oval peel-off sticker that is placed by hand on each and every Chiquita banana. [4]-[9]

1

1 A version of Miss Chiquita from the 1960s

2 The first Miss Chiquita by Dik Browne, 1944

3 The first Chiquita logo, 1947

4 The first Chiquita logo with the blue oval background, an outline version of Miss Chiquita and the distinctive lettering, 1961

5 Chiquita logo with a redrawn version of Miss Chiquita and a name change of the company, 1972

2

3

15

4

5

It was the ideal solution for the problem of how to brand an individual banana without damaging it. Chiquita had already been the first company to brand bananas by wrapping them in paper bearing the Miss Chiquita logo, a practice that had started in 1944. Now for the new sticker, the image of Miss Chiquita was redrawn in a more subtle outline version and the brand name got its own type. [4] Given how perfectly the type fits the oval frame, with its condensed, square and tightly spaced letterforms, it's fair to assume that they were custom-designed for this logo. The sans serif letterforms feature stroke ends with a very subtle broadening, which creates an impression of serifs. This is most pronounced on the top stroke ends of h and u. On the C and the a heavy corners replace the top serifs.

The logo underwent another restyling in 1987. [8] While still dressed in flamenco sleeves with the fruit basket on her head, Miss Chiquita became an elegant Latino lady instead of a cartoon banana. The type of the logo was also updated to reflect the style of the time. The letterforms got a cleaner and sharper look, thanks to the rounded corners and diagonally cut stroke ends. By then, the Chiquita sticker had already become an icon in American culture, and more than two decades on, it remains so. In fact, the stickers were the focal point of a new marketing campaign in 2010 when the company launched a logo design contest. The winning new logo incorporated several adjustments, including in the type. [9] The new letterforms kept the original narrow and square proportions, but the bottom stroke ends were altered to give them a more dynamic look. With the round corners and branched-off stroke ends, the type now subtly resembles the curved shape of a banana. Miss Chiquita was given a bigger smile, making it seem like she is prouder than ever to endorse Chiquita's products. The new logo reflects the company's attempt to modernize its image and its products in order to appeal to a younger generation.

7

8

6 Chiquita advertising, 1960s

7 Chiquita logo without the company
  name, 1980

8 Redesigned Chiquita logo with a new
  Miss Chiquita, new lettering and
  yellow as a second signature colour,
  1987

9 The current Chiquita logo, 2010

9

PERRIER

SINCE 1898

Perrier's story can be traced back to the place where the water springs from: a French town called Vergèze in the Languedoc region. The spring itself is called *Les Bouillens* ('the boiling waters'), gaining its name from the bubbling water that gushes out as if it is boiling. This water was used for therapeutic properties as far back as the Roman Empire and in the mid-19th century as a spa. In 1898, Dr. Perrier became the owner of Les Bouillens and devoted himself to developing a hygienically sealed glass bottle to hold and transport water that contained three times its volume in gas.

In 1903 he got the much needed help of Sir Saint-John Harmsworth, a wealthy British man, who bought the thermal spring and renamed it *Compagnie de la Source Perrier*, after Dr. Perrier. Harmsworth also introduced Perrier's sparkling water in the UK, where everything French was seen as chic at the time. The exceptional water also became popular in the British colonies, and in 1905 Harmsworth even gained the title of Purveyor to the King of England. At that time, Perrier was better known in London, Delhi and Singapore than in Paris. It was launched in the United States in 1967 and soon became a fundamental part of a healthy American lifestyle.

The most distinctive feature of the Perrier packaging is probably its green teardrop-shaped bottle. [1][7] The design wasn't inspired by a water drop, but by the shape of a special Indian wooden club that Harmsworth used to exercise after a leg injury. Harmsworth really was the man responsible for Perrier's strong brand image. Not only did he introduce the new bottle, but also the logotype in which the brand name was drawn. In the first version of the logo, the letterforms are arranged on a curved baseline, which makes the logotype appear to have the shape of an arch. It works

1   Perrier advertisement, 1905

FRENCH NATURAL SPARKLING
TABLE WATER

Perrier

By Special Appointment to H.M. King Edward VII.

By Special Appointment to H.M. King Edward VII.

Source Perrier

"THE CHAMPAGNE OF TABLE WATERS"

PRICES.
Original Cases of
50 Large Bottles 22/-
100 Half Bottles 35/-
100 Quarter Bottles 26/-
Carriage Paid in
United Kingdom.
No charge for Cases.

SAMPLE CASES of PERRIER
containing two large, two small, and two quarter bottles, with the analysis and medical and scientific reports on the water, will be sent carriage paid to any address in the United Kingdom on receipt of a Postal Order for two shillings, addressed to the London Office of PERRIER (Dept. C.N.R.), 45 and 46, New Bond Street, London, W.

PERRIER
can be obtained at all first-class Hotels, Restaurants, Wine Merchants, Stores, etc.

well within the circular paper label with two thinner strips that wrap around the neck of the Perrier bottle. The capital P features a remarkable decorative design. Its narrow and elongated shape is embellished with spurs instead of serifs on the top that look like a crown. The bottom serif is oddly shaped and bears a resemblance to the *fleur-de-lis*, the stylized lily or iris, the quintessential French religious, political and artistic symbol, originally used in heraldry. The lowercase letters e, r and i are drawn in a completely different type style. They look like an intermediate style between more classic seriffed type and the geometrical sans serifs that were being produced all over the Western typographic world and that denoted a new style and approach in type design. [2] (Also see the story about the inspiration by Gill Sans for KitKat's logo, on pp 40-41.)

Over the years, the Perrier letterforms have been altered. Each time, these small changes have made the logotype appear more visually coherent, by blending the type style of the capital P and the lowercase letters. [4]

The current logotype shares strong roots with the original. [5] The concept of the decorative capital P remains, but the shape of the P has been redrawn. It has narrower proportions and more pronounced spurs on the top, and the bottom decorations now face in the other direction. The lowercase letters are drawn in a bold condensed serif type, which relates more to the style of the P. The lowercases feature heavy bracketed serifs, which provide a curved transition between the serif and the main strokes and make the letters stand firmly on their arched baseline. The arch of the r is well pronounced, making the letters easier to read amid the vertical and tightly spaced stems.

20

2

3

4

5

2 Perrier logotype, 1930s
3 Perrier logotype, 1940s
4 Perrier logotype, 1950s
5 Perrier's current logotype
6 Perrier advertisement in London's
   Social Calendar, 1914

After Harmsworth's death, Perrier was bought in 1946 by Gustave Leven, who launched an extensive plan for modernization. In order to boost sales, Leven immediately entrusted Jean Davray with the task of publicizing the Perrier brand. Echoing Perrier's very first advertising slogan, *la princesse des eaux de table* ('the princess of table waters'), Davray came up with a campaign that was built around 'the champagne of table waters'. This poster campaign became the flagship of the advertising strategy. The Perrier slogan that has probably been most famous over the years is *Perrier, c'est fou!* ('Perrier, it's crazy'), also launched by Davray, in 1970. It was used until 1990, and then taken up again in 1995, three years after the brand was acquired by Nestlé. They kept pursuing the same advertising strategy, with the launch of limited editions playing a key role, as did collaboration with artists. This helped the brand to project a bold, offbeat image, while at the same time maintaining its elegance and its hallmark.

Working with artists is something that Perrier started early on, and over the years it has built up an impressive list. The company has boasted names like Jean-Gabriel Domergue, to whom we owe the first 'Perrier Girl' in the 1930s. In the 1950s, French illustrators Villemot, Savignac and Morvan worked on the poster campaigns and Perrier also employed famous writers like Colette, Pierre Mac Orlan and Curnonsky. In 1969, a full colour advert appeared in *Le Figaro* and *France Soir*, signed by Salvador Dali. In the early 1980s Andy Warhol designed a series of 40 or so screenprints that featured the company's teardrop bottles. The posters were used for an ad campaign that eventually won the 1983 *Grand Prix de l'Affiche Française*. [8]

7

Perrier launched a limited edition of specially themed bottles with colourful labels based on this set of screenprints in 2013 in order to celebrate its 150th birthday and to illustrate its bond with the creative arts. The labels bore tiny facsimiles of four of Warhol's Perrier prints and were also etched with various Warholisms, including famous quotes such as: 'In the future everyone will be world famous for 15 minutes'; or 'Art is what you can get away with.' Warhol's signature was scrawled just below the bottles' trademark bulge.

7   Perrier water bottle, 2013
8   *Perrier* by Andy Warhol, MoMA, 1983

OXO

SINCE 1840

24

The Oxo story begins in the 1840s, also known as the 'Hungry Forties' – it was the time when an international food crisis had struck Northern Europe, caused by potato blight. Doctors declared that eating beef would strengthen people's health, but it wasn't available to many. Fortunately there was the chemist Justus von Liebig, who developed a process to extract the beneficial ingredients from meat to make them available to everyone. His beef extract, initially a liquid, was commercialized by the Liebig Company in 1866. It wasn't until the turn of the century that the company introduced the Oxo brand, the name most likely coming from the word 'ox'. The first Oxo cubes were produced in 1910 and welcomed by consumers as they were cheaper than the liquid.

During the course of his career, Justus von Liebig would manage to establish one of the most iconic brands in the United Kingdom. He owes a lot to George Giebert, a brilliant engineer, and to marketeer Charles Gunther, whose marketing vision allowed Oxo to meet its growing competition head on. Gunther's strategy was quite aggressive and revolutionary for the time: he had leaflets printed that were distributed through Oxo's trade outlets; he advertised in the press and on hoardings on an enormous scale; and he introduced gifts that could be exchanged for labels from Oxo bottles. Oxo's first promotional gift was a baby's rattle, in 1902. A year later the name Oxo was beamed from an electric sign in the Strand. Another innovative promotion was sponsorship: Oxo made itself synonymous with health, strength and endurance simply by sponsoring the London to Brighton walk and also the London Olympic Games in 1908 (despite claims by Coca-Cola to being the 'first' commercial sponsor of the Games) where they supplied the runners in the marathon with Oxo

A Good Drink at ALL Times

OXO

JUST ADD HOT WATER

1

1 Oxo cube advertisement, 1940s
2 The Oxo logotype as it appeared on an early advertising poster, 1920
3 Oxo logotype, 1950s
4 Oxo logotype, 1920s – 1930s
5 Oxo logotype, 1960s
6 The current Oxo logotype

2

25

3

4

5

6

drinks to fortify them. During the first half of the 20th century, Oxo was also promoted through enamel shop signs and recipes that were published in newspapers. Gift schemes were again used extensively to promote sales in the twenties; in 1923 some 50,000 Christmas stockings were offered in exchange for 120 cube wrappers. Other give-aways included dolls, cricket bats and footballs.

26 Of course Oxo needed a strong logo to put on all these ads and gifts, not to mention their packaging. The company had a logo designed that turned out to be very recognisable and interesting, helped by the symmetry of the brand name's letters and the combination of round and angular shapes in it. The Oxo logotype plays with these letterforms as visual elements. An Oxo poster from 1920, by the Italian poster artist Leonetto Cappiello, shows the brand name drawn with O's that feature a peculiar style. [2] On each side, the letter contour shows sharp and outward facing thorns that make the letters almost look like two eyes, and yet this works perfectly together with the shape of the X. In a later logotype from the 1930s, [4] the two O's are almost completely circular shapes, with a very small counter that is not situated in the centre, but rather near the top of the letter. This gives the letters a strange modulation, with a very heavy lower half and lighter top. The X that stands between them is completely linear and is made up of two straight strokes that intersect at a 90° angle. The point of intersection is slightly raised above the middle line. The three letters are tightly spaced but because of the negative space on the sides of X this works well; they appear coherent and more as a set of symbols than as three letters.

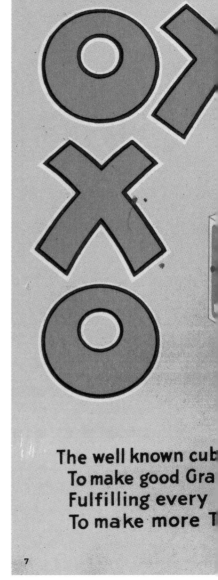

7 Front and back cover from the *Oxo Meat Cook Book*, 1930s

7

The well known cub
To make good Gra
Fulfilling every
To make more T

Meat Cookery! - the OXO way

British section by Elizabeth Craig

The name of the brand also turned out to be a very handy one when the company purchased the iconic Oxo Tower on the south bank of London's River Thames, toward the end of the 1920s. It was originally constructed as a power station for the post office but largely rebuilt to an Art Deco design by Oxo's company architect Albert Moore between 1928 and 1929. His original plans incorporated large illuminated signs to advertise the company's products, but permission for the signs was refused, so Moore decided to build the tower with vertically aligned windows in the shape of a circle, a cross and a circle. [9]

By the second half of the century, Oxo had lost its novelty and become an everyday product in English kitchens. A new marketing approach was necessary. The company turned its status as a regular product in an English family to its advantage and focused its campaign on the importance of family mealtime. One of the customer's gifts that was launched around that time was the Oxo cup. It became particularly popular; almost every household had a few of these cups in the cupboard. The cups are still valued today by lovers of mid-century tableware. In the 1950s the first 'Oxo family' made its television debut featuring in a 'real' advertising soap opera. In fact during the 1960s many people were convinced the Oxo family was actually a real family. By the end of the 1990s, however, the campaign had lost its appeal because it was no longer seen as representative of everyday life, and in September 1999 the family had one last meal together.

For the beginning of the 21st century a new image was promoted with modern television advertising and packaging. At the end of 2009 Oxo re-launched the cubes in a new X shape to aid crumbling. In that same year the company ran a competition to find a new Oxo family. This time they didn't look for actors but for a real family that reflected modern times. The winning family's advert ran during the X factor final. Oxo's current logotype is a continuation of the older ones, with the use of the high bottom-heavy O's, but with the letters redrawn in a less geometrical style. The O's and X with its curved and heavy strokes have a very friendly look, which is enhanced by the black shadow behind the letterforms. The three letters are drawn in a cartoon-like style and stuck together so they almost form one shape. The letters also have a prominent position on Oxo's packaging, with one letter highlighted and shown in large on three of the four sides of the box. They're fun, friendly and in touch with modern-day life. [8]

8 One side of an Oxo box, 2013

9 Oxo tower, London. According to a London legend, the Oxo tower was a smart way to get around a law that prohibited advertising on the banks of the Thames river. The tower was an architectural building so it was not considered an advertisement.

JULES DESTROOPER

SINCE 1886

Belgium's Jules Destrooper biscuits have fans the world over. His first ever biscuit was the Almond Thin, introduced in 1886 and followed soon after by the now legendary Butter Crisp. Jules Destrooper was not only a passionate patissier but also a colonial trader, which enabled him to experiment with exotic spices from Africa and the East and obtain the unique taste of his first biscuit. Today, the business is in the hands of the fourth generation of Destroopers. While the secret family recipes remain the same as those of their great-grandfather, the assortment is regularly extended to embrace the latest trends. The company has also successfully invested in innovations, for example an airtight aluminium packaging method that increased the biscuits' shelf life by up to nine months. This has proved very useful for exports, which have boomed – particularly in Asia – ever since Destrooper became a purveyor to the Belgian royal household.

Of course it's the taste of the cookies that accounts for most of the appeal of the Jules Destrooper name, but the image of the brand as a down-to-earth Flemish family company with authentic, traditional products also resonates with people. That image is sustained by the logo and the quirky letterforms of its type, which convey a certain old-school vibe, grace and elegance. [6] They appear hand-drawn, in the same style as the illustrations of the banners, arrows and the emblems on the box. The capital letterforms of the Jules Destrooper logotype have an almost naïve air to them, with their narrow proportions, a raised middle and spikey concave wedge-shaped serifs. Many letters vary in width, for example L and S appear much wider than T, D and U. Furthermore, the S looks like it is slanted backwards, with a small top and a large open counter space

1   Female employees of Jules Destrooper packing biscuits into boxes, 1886

2   Jules Destrooper's very first packaging, 1886

3   Poster advertisement for Almond Thins, 1930s

1

2

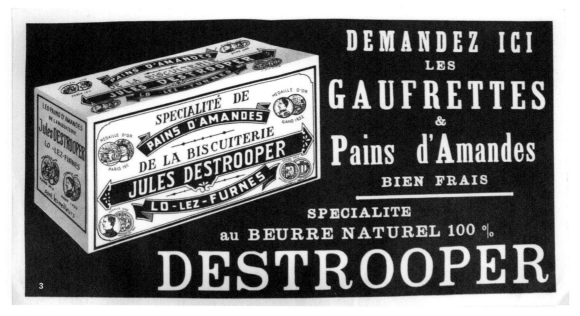

3

on the bottom. The flat curves on the O don't match the full arches on the D, P and R. However, the letters are very carefully drawn, with each kind of letter exactly alike (e.g. all the Os are the same, as are the Es etc), and even the spacing looks mathematically precise, giving the overall impression of a genuine lettertype. 'Specialité de' and 'de la Biscuiterie' are typeset in more conventional types, such as a Clarendon-style Egyptienne typeface [7] and later a neutral sans serif. [5]

The letters were most probably never designed as a single logotype, but instead developed along with the Jules Destrooper packaging. Ever since the brand's launch the cookies have been packaged in a white cardboard box, illustrated with blue type and the medallion emblems. [2][4][5][7] This box has only been changed slightly over the years, for example when images of the crispy waffles were added. In 2012 a hint of gold was introduced to enhance the premium quality of the brand, its rich history and Destrooper's successful entrepreneurship. The packaging now more than ever highlights the brand's values: quality, tradition and authenticity.

4

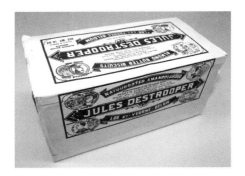

5

4 Jules Destrooper packaging, 1940s
5 Jules Destrooper packaging, at the end of the 20th century
6 Jules Destrooper logo
7 Jules Destrooper packaging, 1920s

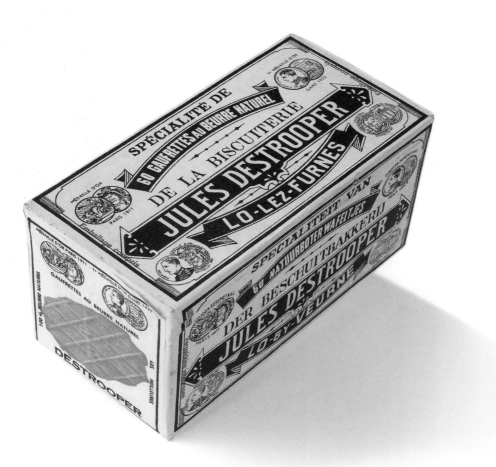

CAMPARI
SINCE 1860

34

Was it a passion for concocting new beverages that drove Gaspare Campari back in 1860 to mix a fair number – some say 20, others 60 – of bitter herbs, aromatic plants and fruits with alcohol and water? Whatever the reason, the man from Novara, Italy succeeded in inventing a drink that has become one of the greatest icons of Italian style. The recipe has remained unchanged to this day. We know that its ingredients include rhubarb, ginseng, bergamot, orange peel and quinine, which adds the specific bitter flavour, but the only person in the world who knows the exact formula is the company's CEO.

Campari has always had an enterprising vision of advertising and a nose for social changes and how they could benefit the business. When cafés started to become more popular (and more numerous) during the Belle Epoque and an aperitif became a social event where people gathered to meet friends, Campari jumped on this shift in bar culture and took a leading role in bar advertising. Bar owners in Italy and Southern France could sell Campari products in their bars in exchange for displaying a Campari advertisement sign. Products like glassware, ashtrays and enamel signs became very popular.

As far back as the 1880s, Campari already had a clear marketing strategy, one that was all about campaigns that focus on artistic images, or rather on an artist's interpretation of the Campari brand. Advertising posters were created by artists such as Marcello Dudovich and Adolfo Magrini, both graphic designers and both regular contributors. Dudovich is also the designer who created the poster of two lovers passionately kissing. [2] It's an iconic image and the first example where drinking Campari, with its

1

1 Advertisement poster by Leonetto Cappiello, 1921
2 Campari advertisement by Marcello Dudovich, 1920

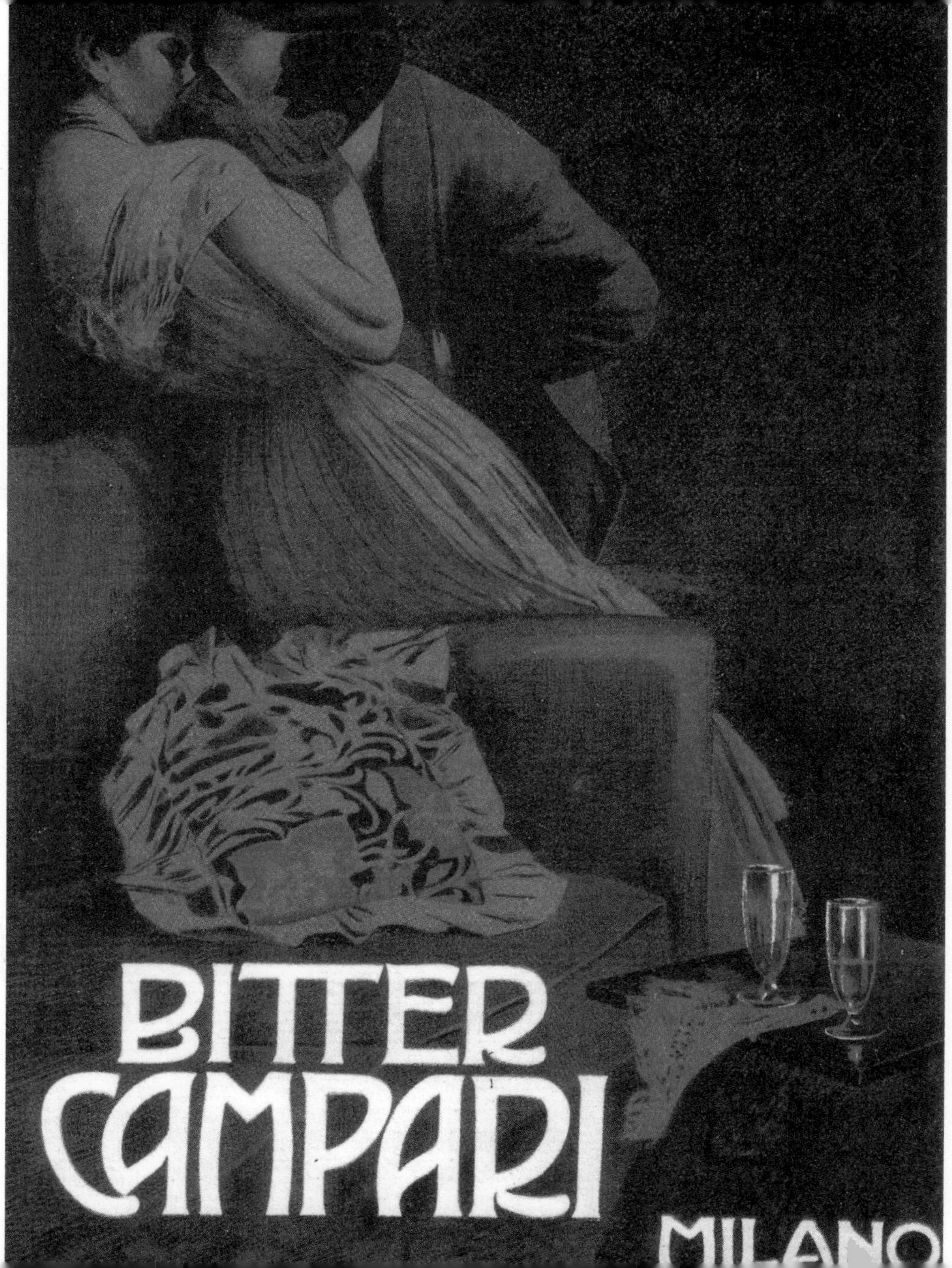

2

distinct deep red colour, was linked with passion and fire; this concept is still an important part of the brand image today.

Another important name to note is that of Marcello Nizzoli, the designer of the Campari poster of 1926. [3] This is the poster on which the Campari logotype appeared for the first time. Until then, the artists had always come up with an appropriate lettering for the posters they were making in the style of the overall design, but this poster shows a logotype that can also stand alone and that was used again in other posters and advertisements. It's not clear who designed the logotype – was it Nizzoli or someone else? Whoever it was, it was a job well done: the sturdy capital letters with heavy wedge shaped block serifs that taper toward the bottom create an instantly recognisable typographic design and work perfectly as a logotype. This is also shown in Bruno Munari's artwork *Declinazione grafica del nome Campari* ('The name Campari in a graphic declination') from 1965, where the logo was broken into smaller blocks and yet still represented the brand's universe and its values. [7] The poster was created for the opening of Milan's first subway line and now belongs to the permanent collection of the MoMA in New York. The current Campari logo still uses the same letterforms, with the only addition being a gold outline to the letterforms; this was most probably added to give a stylish undertone to the logo and thus the brand.

During World War II the Campari advertising campaign was of course suspended. But soon after the war was over, in the late 1940s, the brand launched a new advertising campaign. This time Campari asked avant-garde artist Carlo Fisanotti, better

3

4

3 Advertising poster by Marcello Nizzoli, 1926
4 Advertising poster by Carlo Fisanotti, 1940s
5 Advertising poster by Nino Nanni, 1960

L'OLIMPIONICO DEGLI APERITIVI
L'APERITIVO DEGLI OLIMPIONICI

CAMPARI

known as Fisa, to design the poster, and it became a
resounding success. [4] In recent years, the painters
and graphic artists have been replaced by renowned
photographers such as Mario Testino [9] and Marino
Parisotto. The Campari advertising campaigns that
they have shot are all about the red passion concept.
Just like Testino and Parisotto, all the artists both
before and since are Italian or have strong Italian
roots. This is a conscious choice that adds to the strong
Italian history and atmosphere behind the brand.

Another important element in the brand's image is
clearly the strong bond with the world of art. This is
expressed in many different ways, not just through
commissioning artists to create posters, which speaks
for itself, but also more unexpected projects where
artists have been inspired by Campari. Several artists
from different disciplines have experimented with
the look of the distinctive bottle, for example Raffaele
Celentano, who designed the Campari pendant lamp
for Ingo Maurer in 2001, featuring 10 Campari Soda
bottles. The label has also been a source of inspiration
for artists, most notably in the Campari Art Label
Project that the company set up in 2010 to celebrate
its 150th birthday. Three contemporary international
artists (avaf, Tobias Rehberger and Vanessa Beecroft)
were asked to express their personal interpretation of
Campari in the label. Starting from the essence of the
colour red, the artists created three different artworks
featuring three diverse aesthetic identities. These
labels, which are real works of art, were placed on
bottles and sold to the public as limited editions.
The cherry on the artistic Campari cake was
the opening of the Galleria Campari in 2010 in
recognition of the contribution that art and design has
made to Campari's products over the years.

38

6

6 The current Campari bottle
7 *Declinazione grafica del nome
   Campari,* Bruno Munari, 1965
8 The current Campari logo
9 Salma Hayek by Mario Testino for the
   Campari Calendar, 2007

7

8

9

KITKAT

SINCE 1937

The chocolate-coated wafer that later became KitKat was originally launched in 1935 as Rowntree's Chocolate Crisp. It was developed thanks to an employee at Rowntree's, a confectionary business with a factory in York, who suggested making a snack that 'a man could take to work in his knapsack'. The chocolate bar was rebranded and re-introduced as KitKat in 1937. The origins of the name date back to the late 17th century: it was the nickname of Christopher Catling, the pastry chef of a pie shop frequented at the time by a London literary and political club, the infamous KitKat club.

Rowntree's registered the name KitKat back in 1911, although it wasn't immediately used. When they did start using it in 1937, they also introduced a very straightforward logo. [1] It simply comprised the word 'KitKat' in red, drawn inside a large white oval. The letterforms were also straightforward. The two capital letter K's are drawn with long diagonal legs so that they fit the oval shape. The style of the lowercase letters i, t and a is not dissimilar to the grotesque typefaces that were often issued in Wood Type styles. The letters are heavy, with a square shape, and the outstrokes of the a and the t end fairly high.

The style of the letterforms of the KitKat logotype used today can be traced back to this same period, the 1930s, when the chocolate bar was originally launched. The current logotype has kept the idea of simple letters inside a white oval, but the shapes of these elements have been redrawn to make them rounder and more streamlined. The style of the lettering echoes some characteristics of the typeface Gill Sans, designed by Eric Gill, a renowned graphic artist, type designer and sculptor from the UK. [3] With Gill Sans, the type designer attempted to make the ultimate legible sans serif text face, which needed to function equally well as a text and

1 The very first KitKat wrapper, 1937
2 KitKat's Dark Chocolate blue wrapper, 1942

Kit Kat

CHOCOLATE CRISP

MADE ONLY BY ROWNTREES

4 big chocolate wafers **2**d

2½d KIT KAT

Rowntree's

KIT KAT

Because no milk can be obtained for chocolate manufacture, the Chocolate Crisp you knew in peace-time can no longer be made. Kit Kat is the nearest possible product at the present time.

1

2

as a display typeface. Another motive for releasing Gill Sans was to provide a British counterpart for the popular type families of Futura and Kabel that were launched in Germany during the late 1920s. The inspiration for the Gill Sans design comes from Edward Johnston's typeface for the London Underground, which is still in use today. Its dominant characteristics are the perfect circle of the round letters like the O, o, b and p, combined with straight strokes and little modulation. The capitals are based on Roman square capitals and the lowercase on the humanistic minuscule, which makes the letterforms suitable for typesetting large blocks of text. This marked a break with the previously designed grotesque sans serifs, whose shapes were more square and blocked. Gill Sans has stood the test of time well, with its digital version still widely used today. In the case of the KitKat logo, the design of the i, t and the a look like they are based on a sloped version of Gill Sans's Roman lower case. Distinctive features are the stroke width of the eye of the a, which is lighter than its overhang, and the diagonally closed top of the t. [4]

It is thanks to the logo and its simplicity that KitKat's visual identity has remained so recognisable throughout the years, even during WW II, when KitKat introduced a dark chocolate version – because of the scarcity of food supplies during the war, there wasn't enough milk to produce the milk chocolate coating for the original KitKat wafers. To avoid confusion, the 'dark' KitKat got a blue wrapper. [2] It was only in 1949 KitKat that reintroduced its original milk recipe and red packaging, which is still the brand's signature colour. Today the logo is as recognizable as ever, despite a rebranding when Nestlé took over the brand in 1988, and despite the introduction of a different

3

4

3 Gill Sans Regular and Italic
4 A digitally sloped version of Gill Sans Regular and the KitKat lettering
5 A KitKat wrapper that was especially released for the coronation of Queen Elizabeth of the United Kingdom, 1953

5

packaging in 2001 (the silver foil with an outer paper band in which the chocolate bar had always been wrapped were replaced by plastic flow wrap). [8]

Besides the logo, Nestlé also took over the iconic line 'Have a break, have a KitKat', which was introduced in 1957 and written by the London advertising agency JWT. Nestlé succeeded in trademarking the line in 2005, but only after a 10-year legal battle with rival Mars. Nestlé is now the worldwide owner of KitKat, and the company produces the chocolate bars for almost every country. Sometimes it adjusts the product slightly for individual markets, for example the number of fingers varies, ranging from the half-finger sized KitKat Petit in Japan to the twelve-finger family bars in Australia and France. The United States is the exception to the ownership rule because here the licence to produce KitKat isn't owned by Nestlé but by the Hershey Company; it has been that way since 1970. The different ownership has also meant slight differences in the logo: for many years Hershey used an older lettering for their US KitKat packaging, but in 2002 it adopted the slanted ellipse logo used worldwide by Nestlé.

KitKat is possibly one of the most iconic food brands worldwide. In 2013 it took the No. 1 spot in a list of the 13 most influential candy bars of all time by the magazine *Time*, based on interviews with candy experts and historians to determine which bars made the biggest impact on the chocolate-bar industry (and the world at large). *Time* wrote, 'beyond being the first candy bar to be marketed around sharing, which helped turn chocolate into a social snack, KitKat was also the first to gain a global following. Last year, Google's Android announced its new operating system would be called "KitKat", and in January Tokyo welcomed the first all-KitKat store, featuring flavours like edamame soy bean, purple sweet potato and wasabi.' The story of KitKat in Japan is a particularly interesting one: the snack has become extremely popular because of the resemblance to the Japanese expression *kitto katsu*, which means 'I hope you succeed!' or 'Surely win'. KitKat has become a national good luck charm, all thanks to a Nestlé marketing campaign featuring an edible postcard to wish Japanese students good luck during national exams. Nestlé worked with Japan's postal service to create a mailable KitKat bar with a space for a message that was made available in 20,000 Japan Post outlets. It marked the first time a private company had partnered with Japan Post, and today 'KitKat Mail' is a permanent product offered by the postal service.

6 A limited edition orange-flavoured KitKat, with the new logotype and an orange wrapper, 1995

NEXT PAGE:

7 KitKat chocolate bar with imprinted logos on the bars

8 The Nestlé KitKat wrapper, 2014

FOUR CRISP WAFER FINGERS COVERED WITH ORANGE FLAVOURED MILK CHOCOLATE

MADE WITH NATURAL FLAVOUR FROM REAL ORANGES

Have a Break, Have a...

We appreciate comments or questions
Nestlé Rowntree PO Box No 203
York YO11XY England
Nestlé Rowntree Ireland Blessington Road
Tallaght Dublin 24

 Nestlé ®

℮ 48g

© 1995 Société des Produits Nestlé S.A., Vevey, Switzerland.
Trade Mark Owners.

INGREDIENTS:
Milk chocolate, Wheat flour, Sugar, Vegetable fat, Cocoa mass,
Orange oil 0.4%, Yeast, Raising agent (Sodium bicarbonate),
Salt, Calcium sulphate, Emulsifier (Lecithin), Flavouring.

NUTRITION INFORMATION
100g provides:
Energy 2099 kJ/502kcal
Protein 7.5g
Carbohydrate 59.4g
Fat 26.0g

BEST BEFORE
1 Dec 1996

Store Cool and Dry   Made in the UK

5 000189 127319 >

Beljakovine/ Proteine/ Protéines/ Eiwitten	6,8 g	3,1 g	50 g	6%
Ogljikovi hidrati/ Glucide/ Glucides/ Koolhydraten	60,0 g	27,0 g	270 g	10%
Maščobe/ Lipide/ Lipides/ Vetten	27,7 g	12,5 g	70 g	18%

GUIDELINE DAILY AMOUNT. ⒮ Orientacijska dnevna vrednost temelji na prehrani z 2000 kcal. Osebna potreba variira glede na starost, spol, težo in telesno aktivnost. ⒞ CZE- Cantitate Zilnică Estimată pentru un adult pe porţie. Nevoile nutriţionale individuale pot fi mai mari sau mai mici în funcţie de vârstă, sex, nivel de activitate fizică şi alţi factori. ⒡⒦⒟ Repères Nutritionnels Journaliers pour un adulte avec un apport moyen de 2000 kcal. Repères et portions peuvent varier selon l'âge, le sexe, et l'activité physique. ⒩ Dagelijkse Voedingsrichtlijn voor een volwassene gebaseerd op een gemiddelde behoefte van 2000 kcal. Deze Dagelijkse Voedingsrichtlijn kan variëren afhankelijk van de leeftijd, het geslacht en de lichamelijke inspanning.

Neto količina:

45g ℮

www.kitkat.com

Coût d'un appel local depuis un poste fixe
BE (+32) 02 529 55 25
NL 020-569 5699
www.nestle.com

NA/PER/ POUR/PA/ PRO/POR 45g — OF AN ADULT'S GDA — 234 kcal — 12%

www.nestlecocoaplan.com

Cocoa Plan

Nestlé

Have a break, have a Kit Kat.®

Hrustljavi vafelj v mlečni čokoladi (67,7%). Sestavine: sladkor, pšenična moka, kakavovo maslo, posneto mleko v prahu, rastlinska maščoba, kakavova masa, mlečna maščoba, [...izvod sirotke, manj masten kakav, emulgator (sončnični lecitin), arome, sol, sredstvo za vzhajanje (natrijev hidrogenkarbonat). Prodaja SLO: Nestlé Adriatic Trgovina d.o.o., Šmar[...]a cesta 53, 1000 Ljubljana ⒝ Ciocolată cu lapte (67,7%) cu interior crocant de napolitană. Ingrediente: zahăr, făină de grâu, unt de cacao, lapte praf degresat, grăsime vege[...] masă de cacao, grăsime din lapte, zer praf (din lapte), cacao pudră cu conţinut redus de grăsime (10-12% unt de cacao), emulgator (lecitină de floarea soarelui), arome, sare, agent [...]ânare (carbonat acid de sodiu). Produsul con[...]gluten. Ciocolata cu lapte conţine substanţă [...] de cacao: 29% minim. A se păstra la loc uscat [...]oros. Produs în Germania. Distribuitor: Nestlé [...]nia SRL, Str. George Constantinescu nr. 3, sector [...]ureşti 020339, România. ⒡⒭⒞⒣⒟⒠ Gaufrette [...]tillante enrobée de chocolat au lait (67,7%). [...]ients: su[...]

Uporabno najmanj do konca:/ A se consuma, de preferinţă, până la sfârşitul:/ Lot nr.:/ A consommer de préférence avant fin:/ Ten minste houdbaar tot einde :/ Uporabno najmanj do konca/lot:

L40150734
13 2014

TABASCO

SINCE 1868

Edmund McIlhenny came up with the name Tabasco after inventing his iconic pepper sauce in 1868. It is believed to be a Mexican Indian word that means 'land where the soil is hot and humid'. This definitely describes the climate of Avery Island in Louisiana, where Tabasco is being still produced up to this day, in the family-owned company. Even though it was originally a geographically descriptive word, McIlhenny managed to acquire the exclusive rights for the Tabasco trademark: there is only one sauce that is entitled to call itself Tabasco and that is McIlhenny Co.'s Tabasco Sauce, no other brand can ever use the term in its brand name or communications.

It comes as no surprise that this strong brand name goes hand in hand with a very strong and recognisable logo that hasn't changed since the very beginning, when the company was founded. It consists of green and red type, and a number of curved and straight red lines. [2] There are three different lines written in green; in those we can distinguish two different typestyles: first, the company's name at the top of the logo, which is set in condensed type with hardly any vertical curves, and second 'Tabasco' and 'pepper sauce', which are obviously hand-drawn. This is particularly clear in the letterforms that have an almost clumsy appearance, like the T, which is not symmetrical, and the S, which looks like it is tilted backwards. The curves of the C and the O do not have the same angle, there are many variations in stroke thickness (for example in the U of 'sauce') and there are numerous spacing issues. Despite the fact that all the green type in the circle is hand-drawn, these words have an industrial feel. Then there are the words written in red: these are typeset in Helvetica. Given that this typeface wasn't released until 1957, we must assume that they were either

1

1 Print advertisement, 1940s
2 Tabasco logo

48

updated or added at a later stage. From a type-designing point of view, these letterforms have many imperfections, and it's safe to assume that the unknown designer of the logo wasn't a type designer, but rather a product designer or an engineer. These imperfections, however, are precisely what make this logo look genuine and burst with character, despite the straightforward and sober letterforms.

The logo is consistently applied like a diamond-shaped seal onto a flask. [3] The design of the flask is based on a cologne bottle and has remained almost unaltered over the years. The Tabasco brand offers this distinct shape with the same die-cut label across all its flavour varieties. It's as iconic as the logo. It even plays a role in a number of movies, including Charlie Chaplin's *Modern Times* from 1936. The oldest style of Tabasco bottle known to exist dates back 130 years; it was reconstructed in 2002 from 21 shards of glass that had been dug up by archaeologists at the site of a black-owned Boston saloon.

Just as the Tabasco logo and bottle have hardly changed over the decades, nor has the sauce, which still tastes today as it did a century and a half ago. It's made from just three natural ingredients, red pepper, vinegar and some salt, and is concocted in the same way as it has been ever since the beginning: the peppers are picked at just the right time, the pepper mash is mixed with salt and vinegar, and the mixture is left to age for three years in white oak barrels. Each day, thousands of bottles are made this way, each one containing 720 drops of sauce. From time to time, the company also produces a limited edition of the sauce, which is specially packaged and made available to the public. Paying homage to the original packaging, each bottle of this Family Reserve is sealed with green wax and adorned with a Tabasco Reserve medallion certifying its authenticity.

3

4

3 Print advertisement, 1950s

4 Print advertisement, 1970s

5 Detail from a Tabasco packaging box, distibuted in Belgium

TABASCO® PEPPER SAUCE

Dans votre spaghetti bolognèse
in uw spaghetti bolognese

Dans votre jus de tomate
in uw tomatensap

Dans votre américain
in uw americain

SHAKE WELL

TABASCO®

Tabasco® est le résultat d'un long mûrissement des piments dans les fûts de chêne, ce qui explique son goût et son arôme tout particuliers.

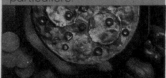

Tabasco® is het resultaat van een lang rijpingsproces in eiken vaten.
Dit verklaart de heerlijke smaak en het bijzondere aroma.

MADE IN U.S.A.
McILHENNY CO.
AVERY ISLAND
LA.
TABASCO®
BRAND
PEPPER SAUCE

57 ml
McILHENNY COMPANY
AVERY ISLAND, LA 70513 USA

51

DUVEL

SINCE 1871

The Belgian Moortgat family have been passionate brewers since 1871; today it is the fourth generation of the family that carries on the tradition. The strong, golden, pale ale Duvel – with its high alcohol content of 8.5% – has been the company's best-known beer throughout the world, with exports shipped to more than 60 countries. It was created after the First World War, during which time Albert Moortgat discovered English ales. He travelled back and forth to England to find the perfect yeast, before finally finding it in Scotland. Even today it is the same yeast that is still being processed, with the same dedication: it takes no fewer than 90 days to finalize the brewing process. The beer was initially called Victory Ale to celebrate the end of the war. During the first tasting session, however, one of the local notables was so excited by the exceptional and pure taste that he cried out: 'This is a real Duvel' (dialect for 'devil', the standard Dutch word being *duivel*). The rest is history.

BROUWERIJ · **MOORTGAT** · BREENDONCK

1

The Duvel logo has undergone several redesigns over the years to reflect the style of the times. An early example of a Duvel logo, from 1948, shows a vivid and illustrative design. The logotype is drawn as a loopy connected script, with irregular letter height and a hand-lettered feel to it. The ample weight of the letterforms and the 3D effect with the white shine and black shadow, together with the playful details of the devil's tails at D and l, make it a cheerful and light-hearted design. **[2, left glass]**

1   The Moortgat brewery in Breendonk, Belgium
2   Re-issued Duvel glassware with prints of retro logotypes, 2011

In 1957, the logo was redesigned. **[3]** This time, the letters were written in a blackletter typeface. The type, known as Textura, dates back to the Middle Ages and was used throughout Western Europe from approximately 1150 to the 17th century, and as late as the 20th century in the German language. Blackletter was developed in response to more and more books being published and the need for a writing form that could be produced faster. The type style emerged from the Carolingian minuscule, a script created under the patronage of the Emperor Charlemagne as a calligraphic standard in Europe between approximately 800 and 1200. The letterforms of the blackletter style are typically tall and narrow, with a definite vertical stress. The stroke of the broad nib pen is clearly detectable in the sharp, straight and angular strokes. The lines tend to break at the curves and at the point where two strokes connect with each other. In the case of the Duvel logo, the letterforms were drawn by hand: the e looks a bit quirky and the spacing between the last three letters could be a little looser.

While staying faithful to the blackletter style, Duvel chose in 1964 to make some adjustments. **[4]** This is most noticeable in the e where the vertical lines became much stronger compared to the more calligraphic and slightly unstable e of the 1957 logo. The capital at the beginning of the word became a lowercase d and the l gained a loop at the top. The upper line of the letters fits perfectly with the shape of the Duvel heraldry that was also added to the design at this stage. As well as the logo itself, important elements of the brand's identity include the tulip-shaped glasses that were introduced by the third Moortgat generation in the late '60s. Reminiscent

54

3

4

5

6

3 Duvel logotype, 1957

4 Duvel logotype, 1964

5 Duvel beer bottle

6 Duvel's signature tulip shaped glass

of the way wine is tasted, the shape of the glass helps to release all the aromas. Another feature is an engraved D on the bottom of the glass, which creates the typical sparkling in the beer. [10] Over the course of the following years, limited editions of these Duvel glasses have occasionally been issued, each time with variations of the Duvel logo; needless to say, they are real collector's items. Between 2010 and 2012, Duvel launched a set of glasses that were created in collaboration with international artists like Eley Kishimoto, Dutch graphic artist Parra and Belgian graffiti artist Dennis Meyers. This resulted in a collection of designs, often with a typographic approach. [9]

With another redesign in 1971, the logo reverted back to a script type that can be considered as an intermediate form between the playful script of 1957 and the more severe blackletter. [7] For example, the u and the v have instrokes that resemble the construction pattern of the blackletter letters. With the swash capital D and the cheeky line under the letters, this style of lettering does not seem entirely fitting for the product. When the logo underwent another redesign, it reverted to the blackletter style, with the letters redrawn and more balanced, each with an equal stroke width and a heavier weight. [8] They are clearly based on a historic style, but well-executed and elegant. This is the Duvel logo that is still used today. It's interesting to see how it proves to be timeless and so apt for the Duvel brand, even with a design of letters that can be traced back to the medieval blackletter, a historical and mostly abandoned script.

56

7

8

7 Duvel logotype, 1971

8 The current Duvel logotype

9 Duvel limited edition glasses, by Amsterdam lettering artist Letman (2012), graffiti artist Denis Meyers (2011) and illustrator Stefan Glerum (2011)

10 The typical Duvel sparkle

9

10

LU

SINCE 1850

58

The name LU originates from a blossoming love affair in Nantes, France, in 1850. A baker named Monsieur Jean-Romain Lefèvre married his girlfriend and business partner, Mademoiselle Pauline-Isabelle Utile. Together they passionately created their biscuits, approaching each biscuit as a work of art and proudly placing the initials of their last names on the result, like every great artist does.

In time, the son of Lefèvre and Utile took over the company and in 1886 he created the *Véritable Petit-Beurre*, the famous rectangular-shaped biscuit with 52 teeth. Louis Lefévre also had a rethink about the packaging: his vision was that the packaging needed to be visually appealing in order to whet the appetite. The company would pursue that vision pretty far by starting to collaborate with artists to create posters and advertisements, inspired by the French sense of style and fine taste. Among those figures were the Art Nouveau artist Alphonse Mucha and the fashion illustrator René Gruau.

Of course, typography also plays an important role when it comes to making packaging and advertisements appealing. True to the vision of its founder, the company LU has always paid attention to the lettering of the LU logo. In the case of LU's *Véritable Petit-Beurre* biscuit, type is even more important as it's one of the few food products that show type on the actual product. This distinctive biscuit, with its four corners to nibble at and its 52 teeth, is part of French heritage; it's like a monument. It uses an imprinted hand-drawn type that is very decorative with bifurcated serifs, reflecting LU's mid-19th century roots. In 1897 this type style was to inspire the then celebrated painter and illustrator Firmin Bouisset, who was commissioned to design the image for the brand's signature cookie *Le Petit Ecolier* (or 'The Little Schoolboy'): he painted not only the school-

1 *Le Petit Ecolier* by Firmin Bouisset, 1897

boy but also an early monogram with low-contrast type, featuring oversized bifurcated serifs. [1]

Art and design continued to be highly valued by the fourth generation of the Lefévre-Utile family. In 1957, a new logo was commissioned from Raymond Loewy. [2] Loewy is one of the best-known industrial designers worldwide and worked on a large number of important projects for different industries. His designs include a Greyhound bus, railroad designs, Coca-Cola vending machines and logos for Shell, BP and Lucky Strike. He was nicknamed 'The Man Who Shaped America'. Remarking on his task to redesign the LU Petit Beurre package and the logo, he likened it to 'redesigning the French flag'. Loewy ended up creating a logotype that has become iconic: a red rectangle with the two letters in white. The letterforms have a clean sans serif, very narrow and enlongated shape. The strength of this logotype is that the letters appear more like vertical shapes than readable letters.

As iconic as it may have been, the LU logo was in need of a makeover in the 1990s. The overall proportions of the letters remained the same, but small pointy serifs were added. The red rectangle also gained an additional element, with the suggestion of a peel-off sticker that shows the yellow underside. [3] In 2011 a more explicit update of the logo was carried out. The curled background was exchanged for a trapezium-shaped red plane and extra dimension was created with drop shadows behind the type. The vertical stress was discarded and the letters became heavier with rounded corners. According to the branding agency Dragon Rouge, the letterforms communicate taste; at the same time the LU logo creates an umbrella for the logos of the sub-brands. [4]

60

2

2 LU logo by Raymond Loewy, 1957
3 LU logo, 1990s
4 LU logo by Dragon Rouge, 2011
5 A painted advertising sign of Lefèvre-Utile, on the wall of the bakery *Du pain et des idées* in Paris

3

4

5

DOUWE EGBERTS

SINCE 1883

Douwe Egberts has been in the coffee roasting business for more than 250 years. It all started when Egbert Douwes and his wife Akke Thysses started selling coffee and other groceries in their tiny shop *De Witte Os* ('The White Ox') in Joure, a rural village in Friesland in the northern part of The Netherlands. Their mission was to sell products that are 'the pleasures of daily living', such as coffee, tea and tobacco. Their son Douwe Egberts took over the store, and business started booming as he sold the products all over the country. His descendants continued along this path and in the nineteenth century Douwe Egberts became an established brand name and a company with a strong business sense. Also in the following century, the company managers proved they had a nose for business opportunities, for example during WWII: stocks of coffee, tobacco and tea depleted rapidly and there was no way to acquire new supplies. A coffee substitute was therefore sold, consisting of barley, peas, beans, chicory and tulip. Douwe Egberts produced this coffee substitute under the brand name Fama, which became so popular that it continued to be sold until 1952, long after regular coffee made its way back onto the market.

Douwe Egberts has always marketed its products very well. The famous red seal that is still an important part of the packaging today refers to the wax stamp from earlier times. As for the circle with DE in it, this was discussed for the first time during advertising meetings in 1924. [4] Its first appearance dates back to 1925, [5] when it was used on tobacco packaging. During the following years the seal took on many guises, for example in green, yellow, gold and blue, each used as a code for a different quality of product. In 1932, the colour-coded seals were replaced by one single red seal, and the quality levels were differentiated by the terms 'red brand',

1 Packaging Douwe Egberts dessert coffee, 1954
2 Packaging Douwe Egberts dessert coffee, 1966

MOULU

POIDS NET 250 GRS.

Douwe Egberts
Café Dessert Extra

Torréfaction de Cafés

D·E

DESSERT

DOUWE EGBERTS
ANVERS

Depuis 1753

R.C.A. 106.942

1

GEMALEN   MOULU

250 GRS

Douwe Egberts
Koffie · Café

Kwaliteit · Qualité

D·E

DESSERT

DOUWE EGBERTS
ANTWERPEN · ANVERS

Anno 1753

H.R.A. 106.942 R.C.A. - IMPORT

2

'blue brand' and 'gold brand'. The type of the DE monogram in the red seal has hardly changed over the years. It shows a decorative style of titling capitals that was very popular in the first decades of the 20th century, originally derived from Art Nouveau type styles. [6]-[10]

Besides the seal, the packaging of all Douwe Egberts' products also features a female figure. This 'Coffee Lady' is pictured as a Frisian peasant woman, connecting the brand to its region of origin. [1][2] In 2002, then Marketing Director F. Reefman decided to re-design the Coffee Lady to make the brand more visible, more surprising and more distinctive. She was reshaped as the 'Aroma Lady', with the lines of her face formed by the strokes of the coffee vapour, creating an ethereal and contemporary look.

In 21st century, Douwe Egberts underwent a major rebranding when the coffee and tea brands were split off from the parent company Sara Lee. At the time the brand was finding it difficult to maintain a strong position in an increasingly saturated market. Douwe Egberts was in danger of falling far behind the competition, which was focusing on marketing concepts based on coffee's origins, mellow moods, fairtrade and sustainability. The core strengths of Douwe Egberts were mainly perceived as being taste and functionality; the brand of course needed to encompass this, but it also needed to add the feel of connoisseurship and an emotional appeal. A new marketing strategy was set up that was all about focusing on the rich history of the brand. First of all the company got a new official name that immediately highlights its founding year and thus its long history: D.E Master Blenders 1753. [3] The new design of the logo, packaging and advertisements also aimed to show the brand as one with a rich history, even though it uses fresh contemporary graphics to express this. The D.E seal was redrawn as a clean geometrical rounded octagonal shape and the D.E initials and wordmark 'Master Blenders' set in a contemporary condensed sans serif type with roots in the industrial and utilitarian sans serifs of the 19th century, [10] which were mainly used for printing ephemera like leaflets and advertisements. The historic roots also come through with the reintroduction of the coffee lady, but this time as a clean vector illustration that fits the present-day approach of Douwe Egberts.

3

3 The current D.E Masterblenders logo
4 Douwe Egberts red seal logo, 1924
5 Douwe Egberts red seal logo, 1925
6 Douwe Egberts red seal logo, 1928
7 Douwe Egberts red seal logo, 1930
8 Douwe Egberts red seal logo, 1930
9 Douwe Egberts red seal logo, 1978
10 Douwe Egberts red seal logo, 2001
11 Douwe Egberts red seal logo, 2010
12 Douwe Egberts red seal logo, 2012

4

5

6

7

8

9

10

11

12

CAMPBELL'S

SINCE 1869

The Campbell's Soup Company was formed in 1869 when Joseph Campbell, a fruit merchant, and Abraham Anderson, an icebox manufacturer, produced Campbell's Tomato soup for the very first time. It became an instant success because it was cheap, easy to prepare and tasty. Other products that they produced included canned tomatoes, vegetables, jellies, condiments and minced meats. The most important innovation in the brand's history was made in 1897 by chemist John T. Dorrance who came up with the formula for condensed soup. He decided to take out the main ingredient, water, in order to lower the transportation costs. He became the president of the company in 1914, when he bought out the Campbell family.

The label that was affixed to the very first condensed soup cans in 1897 was orange and blue, but just a year later it was changed to red and white, which are still Campbell's signature colours today. It was Herberton Williams, one of Campbell's executives, who came up with the idea after watching the Cornell University football team play a game in their brilliant new red and white uniforms; those uniforms made such a strong impression on him that he convinced the company to adopt the red and white as their own and to change the labels on the cans of soup. To this day, the layout of that can with its red and white design has changed very little. [1] [3] The typographic design of the Campbell's brand name features brush-style lettering. The script is very similar to Joseph Campbell's own signature, which may have been used as a basis for the label script. It was probably designed, according to corporate archivist Jonathan Thorn, to appeal to the housewife of the time. 'It was intended to look like cursive handwriting of the day that one would find on handwritten recipes,

1 Campbell's soup can, 2012

equating to "Homemade".' The lettering style resembles the style of sign lettering, which was still a much practised craft in 1910, when the Campbell's logo was created. The Campbell's lettering shows a few quirky letterforms, like the capital C with its two curls and swash loop at the top. Also the b has an unusual shape with the bottom stroke that goes inwards instead of connecting with the next letter e. The construction of that e resembles the shape of a calligraphic capital E. These unconventional features make the design recognisable and allow it to stand out as a logotype. [2]

   Besides the Campbell's logo, the soup cans show a variety of typographic styles. Below the brand name, there is the word 'condensed' set in wide, modern sans serif capitals, and in the centre of the soup cans there is a metallic gold medal seal; it's the Gold Medallion for Excellence that Campbell's was awarded at the 1900 Paris Exhibition. Under the medal the variety of the soup (e.g. tomato, asparagus, clam chowder etc.) is set in a neutral, bold, condensed sans serif style, again in capitals. Finally, at the bottom the word 'soup' features old-style heavy capitals with block serifs and inline decorations. [1]

Campbell's Soup has invested heavily in advertising since its inception and many of its promotional campaigns have proven to be valuable in the Americana collectible advertising market. The first Campbell's advertisements date back to 1899, when advertising was still relatively rare in the US. John Dorrance decided to place ads on New York City streetcars, and by so doing managed to increase sales in New York by 100%. Perhaps best known are the Campbell Kids: jolly rosy-cheeked children who were pictured in ads enjoying a bowl of Campbell's Soup.

Campbell's

2

68

2 Campbell's logotype

3 Campbell's tomato soup wrapper, 2011

4 Campbell's Soup can in an 'Andy Warhol version', distributed in the UK, 2012

5 Illustration of a Campbell's Kid, carrying a soup can, by Grace Wiederseim Drayton

69

4

5

They were designed in 1904 by Grace Wiederseim Drayton, an illustrator and writer, who added some sketches of children to her husband's advertising layout for a Campbell's condensed soup. [5] The advertising agents loved the sketches and chose them as trademarks. The kids became so popular that there were dolls made after them, and they earned their 'mother', Grace Wiederseim Drayton, a position as an illustrator for Campbell's ads for nearly 20 years. In addition to collectible advertising, the company has also had notable commercial sponsorships. Among these was Orson Welles's *The Campbell Playhouse*, a sponsored continuation of the radio drama *The Mercury Theatre on the Air* that started in 1938. Another great marketing achievement is the *M'm! M'm! Good!* advertising song, which generations of Americans can hum. It was introduced on the radio in 1930.

The Campbell's logo became truly immortal in 1962, when pop artist Andy Warhol turned Campbell's red and white soup can into an icon of American popular culture. His artwork *Campbell's Soup Cans* consists of 32 canvases, each portraying a Campbell's Soup can – one for each soup flavour that was available at the time. [6] Warhol, a commercial illustrator who became a successful author, publisher, painter and film director, showed *Campbell's Soup Cans* in his first one-man gallery exhibition in Los Angeles. This exhibition marked the West Coast debut of pop art. The commercial subject of this artwork caused a lot of resistance because of the combination of the semi-mechanized process, the non-painterly style and the commercial subject. The work was said to affront the fine art values, technique and philosophy of abstract expressionism, which was the dominant art movement in the US during the post-war period. This controversy led to a great deal of debate about the ethics of the Pop Art movement, but also helped Warhol distinguish himself from other rising pop artists and made the logo and visuals of Campbell's Soup firmly set in the collective memory. Campbell's even included Warhol's work when they launched a limited series of soup cans in Pop Art style for the artwork's 50th anniversary. [4]

6

6 *Campbell's Soup Cans*, Andy Warhol, 1962

MAILLE

SINCE 1747

72

Maille is one of the oldest brands still in use today. It all started with an antiseptic vinegar invented in an effort to end an outbreak of the plague in the south of France in 1720. Its creator, Antoine Maille, went on to establish his reputation as the greatest vinegar and mustard maker of all time. In 1747 his son founded the house of Maille in Paris and created the Maille Dijon Original mustard, which is to this day still prepared using the same recipe and techniques. In the 1760s Maille was named the official vinegar supplier and distiller to the Majesties of Austria and Hungary, and later to the King of France. In 1771 he became the official supplier of Catherine II of Russia.

Maille clearly has a lot of history and it wears its heritage with pride. This is reflected not least in the brand's logo, which states that Maille products are made in France and also comprises a decorative stamp with *depuis 1747* ('since 1747'), ornate heraldry featuring two angels and the Maille brand name underneath. [4][5] These were features not only of the original logo, but also of the one that was revised in 2009 and is in use today.

    The capital letters of the original logo were drawn in Tuscan type, a style that was very popular in 19th century England and suited the excessively ornamented style of the Victorian Era. This period was characterized by its interpretation and eclectic revival of historic styles combined with Eastern influences. Tuscan is a style characterized by contrasted letterforms with rounded or pointed terminals that have bifurcated or trifurcated serifs (the serifs are divided into branches). The style of the Maille logo was a rather modest version since it is also possible to have mid-stem decorations and decorative embellishments. [5]

1

1 Maille mustard packaging
2 Maille shop on the Place de la Madeleine in Paris

The Tuscan type style dates back to ancient Rome, to inscriptional letters designed by the calligrapher Philocalus in the middle of the fourth century. The characteristic branched serifs are even believed to symbolically represent a fishtail to the early Christians. Although the Tuscan style played second fiddle to the dominant classical style in Victorian England, it was nonetheless designed and distributed by the best-known 19th century English type foundries and printers. Many American Wood Type manufacturers picked up the Tuscan style, which stayed popular until the end of the 19th century. While the regional and historical roots of the typographic style may not marry completely with Maille's origins, the Tuscan style gives the logo a regal tone, which is rather fitting for a brand with such a rich history.

In 2009 the brand identity of Maille was slightly revised. The revisions maintained the strong link with the brand's history, while increasing the importance of the epicurean and sensorial values. The original logo with its traditional feeling, for example the black and gold codes with Tuscan style lettering, [5] gave way to a logo block that softened into a wave shape [6]. It still very clearly represents the style of the original founder of Maille, but added to that it hints at the smoothness of the products. The product range has become broader to account for modern tastes, for example introducing speciality top-quality vinaigrettes and adding the tagline 'Fine Gourmets', typeset in a calligraphic style, to emphasise the authenticity of the recipes. To feel that authenticity and the history of Maille come alive, you can visit one of the two beautiful Maille boutiques in France. The original shop that opened in 1845 is located in Dijon, Burgundy, a region renowned for its mustard. The other was set up in Paris in 1996. [2]

3

4

3 The Maille product range
4 The Maille emblem
5 The original Maille logotype
6 The current Maille mustard label

5

6

KELLOGG'S

SINCE 1898

In 1898 Will Keith Kellogg accidentally flaked wheat berry while he was attempting to make granola. He was working at that time as an assistant to his brother, a doctor at the famous Battle Creek Sanitarium in Michigan. The patients savoured this novelty so much that W.K. and his brother soon received orders from all their friends and family. By 1906, Kellogg's Corn Flakes had become widely available to the public.

W.K. Kellogg is one of those company founders who has built up an internationally successful major brand. In the early years was already advertising his products, in a way that was very unique at that time: he distributed free samples to convince customers of the quality of the corn flakes. In 1910 Kellogg's took billboard advertising to a whole new level, when they had built an electrical sign of 32 metres high on a roof on Times Square in New York City. It was the largest electrical sign known to man at the time. Other advertising strategies included the organisation of a children's art contest, of which the best entries would be used in the advertisements, and the creation of mascottes to go on the packaging, like Cornelius the rooster for the regular corn flakes and Tony the tiger for the frosted flakes. [4]

Also, to help consumers distinguish his brand from competition, W.K. Kellogg put his signature on each Corn Flakes packaging, to show that it was a genuine Kellogg product. [1] A modified version of this signature would later become the company logo. It was uniformized in the late 1910s, when the multiple versions that were being used got replaced by one standard logotype. The script type has a dynamic and strong handwritten feel, because of the full and round letterforms. It looks like the imaginary person who wrote the logotype always lifted his pencil

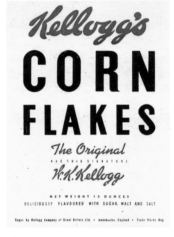

1

1 One of Kellogg's first packaging boxes, from around 1910, with the original signature of W.K. Kellogg below and the first Kellogg's logotype at the top

2 Kellogg's advertisement of an American boy scout with a box of Kellogg's, 1917

Ask the American Boy Why He Prefers Kellogg's—

These are the flakes that are delicately toasted and thin—the original toasted corn flakes, tender and crisp, with that appetizing "come to breakfast" flavor you can't mistake or forget.

W. K. Kellogg

KRUMBLES is Kellogg's *all-wheat* food.
Every single tiny shred is thoroughly toasted.

Kellogg's
TOASTED
CORN
FLAKES

between the second l and the o and between the two g's. When the Kellogg's wordmark got an update in 1970, it was only on the level of the letterforms. **[7]** The capital K was redrawn with the legs disconnected to the stem, and improvements were made on the shapes of the letters like the top of 'g' and the apostrophe. The average customer would not even have noticed the alterations.

The Kellogg's logotype has gone through occasional minor changes through the years, but the overall dimensions and look remained the same for 106 years. **[6][7]** Even when Kellogg's launched a bright, colourful new corporate image for all it's cereal brands in 2000, the logotype stayed the same. In fact, based on marketing research, a design was chosen in which the K-logo was highlighted – the same logo that was based on the original signature of W.K. Kellogg. The big advantage of bringing out this K-logo even more was that it was a protectable brand image. Like the founder of the company allready knew: other competitors would not be able to imitate it. Having decided on the new corporate brand icon, the designers had to incorporate it into the design of the packaging for all 29 individual brands. The latest computer technology was used to digitally generate the artwork and the familiar characters such as Snap, Crackle and Pop, Captain Rik and Tony the Tiger were re-drawn in a more contemporary style. For each product the image was designed to wrap around the box and each side, including the bottom have also been given a strong branded look. It was essential not to alienate consumers with radical new designs and it was important to maintain the individuality of each brand. Frosties, for example, kept Tony the Tiger, the

3

3 Kellogg's Rice Krisp packaging, distributed in the Netherlands, 1963
4 Advertisement for Kellogg's Frosties with Tony the Tiger, 1970

familiar blue background and typeface, [5] while Corn Flakes still radiates sunshine and keeps the red and green cockerel.

The same version of the well-known signature logo that was used – with some very slight changes once in a while – for 106 years was finally updated in 2012, as part of a major rebranding project, because the Kellogg's brand began to lose its way as the company diversified its product offerings. The rebranding focused mainly on the websites and the design of the packaging and advertisements, but also all the letters of the logotype were redrawn with slightly different proportions and some of the thicker parts of the signature have been made smoother. [8] The most noticeable change is that all letters, except K, are now connected. According to the branding agency Interbrand, this 'implies continuity—a metaphor for a familiar, ever-present brand in the day-to-day lives of millions of people all over the world'. The trademark K has changed the least, with the most noticeable alteration being that the stem is now connected to the rest of the letter. The changes to the logotype will probably go largely unnoticed by most Kellogg's costumers. And that is somewhat intentional, as the update is part of a marketing push that is said to refresh the brand 'in ways consumers will continue to relate to'.

5

6

5 The current Kellogg's Frosties packaging with a redrawn Tony the Tiger.
6 An early Kellogg's logotype, 1920
7 Kellogg's logotype, 1970
8 Kellogg's redrawn logotype, 2012

COCA-COLA

SINCE 1886

Coca-Cola is the classic example of how good marketing can turn something as simple as a soda brand into a global icon. Its logo is one of the most identifiable in the history of marketing and logo design. Since the brand's foundation at a soda fountain in a pharmacy in Atlanta in 1886, Coca-Cola has not stopped expanding and has become the most popular drink in many countries across the globe. Until 1905, it contained extracts of cocaine as well as the caffeine-rich kola nut – hence the name. The inventor, a chemist called John Pemberton, sold the liquid as a medicine. At that time, Coca-Cola wasn't yet a marketed brand, and the name was just typeset in chunky slab serif capital letters to distinguish it from other plain text. [2]

In 1887, Dr. Pemberton's bookkeeper Frank Mason Robinson came up with an alternative look for the brand's name. He wrote the words 'Coca-Cola' in flowing Spencerian script, [3] a style that was used in the United States in the second half of the 19th century and up to the 1920s. It was considered the American standard writing style for business correspondence prior to the typewriter. Various existing forms of handwriting were used as an inspiration to develop this oval-based penmanship style. The Spencerian script could be written very quickly and legibly and served for both elegant personal letter-writing as well as formal business correspondence. The handwriting style is characterized by oval letterforms with an even parallel slope and an overall skilful appearance. The text colour is rather light because the writing is done with a pointed pen. Capitals and outstrokes feature decorative embellished swashes and curls. The Coca-Cola logo by Robinson does not show a very high level of skilfulness, with different slope angles in the o, the c and the a, and an

1 Coca-Cola print advertisement, 1905

2 The first Coca-Cola wordmark, 1886

3 The first Coca-Cola logotype, drawn by F. M. Robinson, 1887

4 Coca-Cola logotype, 1893

5 Coca-Cola logotype, 1901

6 Coca-Cola logotype, 1940s

AFTER
EXERCISE
DRINK
Coca-Cola
DELICIOUS   REFRESHING
5¢ AT ALL FOUNTS
AND SOLD IN BOTTLES 5¢

1

COCA-COLA.

2

Coca-Cola

83

3

Coca-Cola

4

Coca-Cola

5

Coca-Cola

6

irregular base line. The curve of the swash of the first capital C also looks a bit bumpy. Nonetheless, it is this version of the logo that was registered as a trademark in 1887. However, it could not be copyrighted since it was in a form of handwriting that was actively practised at the time.

In 1888, the recipe was sold to Asa Candler, an American entrepreneur who decided to sell it as a drink and made a vast fortune from it. In 1892, $12,000 was spent on advertising the brand. Since then, Coca-Cola advertising campaigns have been an integral part of American visual popular culture. A very well-known example that shows how Coca-Cola has influenced pop culture is the image of the jolly Santa Claus with his white beard and red suit: created by Coca-Cola's illustrator Haddon Sundblom in 1931, for most people this is *the* Santa-Claus. [10]
    The logo was updated in 1893; the letterforms were adjusted and balanced. The contrast in the letters was increased, the swashes in the capital Cs were given more elegant outlines, and the outstroke of the second C gained some weight in the form of a little flag. [4] Still, logos were reproduced by hand in those days, either traced over or just hand-painted for advertisement signs. That's why there were probably more than a dozen different versions of the Coca-Cola logo circulating during the first decades of the 20th century.

The logo that we know today was designed in the early 1940s. [6] The letterforms were reshaped, for example the thin parts of the curved letters gained some weight; this reduced the contrast, which in turn made the logo more legible in smaller sizes. The proportions of the letters were adjusted and the slope angle became steeper, resulting in narrower and more elegant letterforms. It is only at this stage that a clear and consistent Coca-Cola logo is finally in place, one that is used consistently in different contexts. Coca-Cola's current logo still features the same letterforms, but several marketing campaigns have added different support graphics, like waves, shields and taglines to the style guide. The strength of the Coca-Cola logo is that it has strong roots in the time when the product was invented and that, for the average consumer, the logo has hardly changed over the years.

7

8

7 Coca-Cola coupon, 1916

8 Coca-Cola can, 2013

9 Coca-Cola bottle, 2013

10 Coca-Cola print advertisement featuring Santa Claus, 1940

9

10

85

HEINZ

SINCE 1869

86

Henry John Heinz established the Heinz company in 1876, in Pittsburgh, USA. The company produced and sold bottled and jarred condiments and sauces. From the very beginning, ketchup has been its top-selling product. Heinz valued the quality of his products, but he also turned out to be a marketing wizard who understood consumers well. One of his decisions was to launch the famous '57 varieties' slogan, which can still be read on all Heinz ketchup bottles today. The company did not actually distribute 57 different kinds of products, but Heinz came up with this number as a sales strategy – he was inspired during a train ride in 1892 when he saw a publicity display advertising shoes that could be bought in 21 different models. He chose the figure 57 because it combined his lucky number (5) and that of his wife (7). [1] [2]

Heinz was aware of the impact of quality packaging. Even in the early days, the company had an in-house design studio where colourful labels for the packaging and advertisements were developed and then printed using lithography. The Heinz ketchup bottle itself has always been very important too. The design of this iconic octagonal bottle with its long curved neck was patented back in 1890. [3] For Henry John Heinz, a glass bottle stood for confidence, honesty and transparency. The paper label stuck on the glass bottles has its own history. Created around 1889 in the shape of a keystone, it probably refers to the roots of the brand and its founder, since Pennsylvania is known as the keystone state. The keystone label is still used on all Heinz products today. This repetition helps to build a strong visual identity, no matter the type, shape or colour of the packaging. A glass ketchup bottle and a blue can of Heinz's baked beans have a completely different look, but they appear visually coherent

1

1 Heinz's '57 varieties' logo

2 A rooftop sign of the number 57, on the Heinz factory, Pittsburgh, USA

3 Left: Heinz ketchup bottle, 1889
   Right: Heinz ketchup bottle, 1892

4 Different shapes of ketchup bottles, 1890 – 2008

5 Heinz label with a pickle as logo, 1897

2

3

4

5

because of the uniform labels and type. It also shows that Heinz highly values, and is proud of, its history. [16 → p. 94-95]

It's remarkable that both the packaging and the logo have changed so little over the years. The label has always contained two main typographic elements: the company's name on the top and the name of the product in the middle of the label. From the very first label, the design and the type have been rather straightforward. In 1903, a fairly narrow sans serif type style adorned the label. [6] The spacing looks a little inconsistent because the label wraps around the sides of the bottle. Heinz's company name is drawn in narrow seriffed letters, reflecting the style of the early 1900s, with the raised middle line in the H and the E. The middle bar of the E and the bottom stroke of the Z are curved and wavy. In 1908, the letters of 'tomato ketchup' were redrawn, adding Art Nouveau influences. [7] A light type style is used, with thin spikey serifs, such as the angled serifs on the bar of the T, the M with full top serifs and a curved, raised middle point and the bottom of the C that is curled inward. From 1948 on, the Heinz labels show a heavier type style, which looks like an intermediate style between the 1903 and 1908 examples. [8] The letterforms have a very low contrast and small, subtle serifs that emphasise the outward movement of the stroke, such as on the bottom serifs of the A. The 'Heinz' type was also updated and is consistent with the style of the rest of the type, only much narrower to fit the top part of the keystone shape. The Z features two quirkily cut corners.

6

7

6 Heinz ketchup bottle, 1903
7 Heinz ketchup bottle, 1908
8 Heinz ketchup bottle, 1948
9 Heinz ketchup bottle, 1960
10 Heinz ketchup bottle, 2000
11 Heinz ketchup bottle, 2008

8

9

10

11

The Heinz story is an impressive example of thorough branding design. Even during the Great Depression, the company, led at the time by the founder's son Howard, invested a lot of money in print advertising, radio commercials and market research. It turned out to be a smart tactic since Heinz was one of the first great companies to rid itself of debt and start to see a pickup in sales. In 1948, a new bottle design was introduced. The overall proportions remained the same, but the edges of the eight sides of the bottle were smoothed out and the bottom made to curve inward. An adjustment to the type styles on the labels followed a little later, in 1960; all the type styles were given the same proportions, and these are still used to the present day. [9] Even the plastic bottles we know today (the first one was launched in 1983) are designed to resemble the iconic glass bottle. [14]

The letters of the Heinz labels now exist as a digital typeface as well. It is not only used as a display typeface on the Heinz company website, the company also went one step further by launching its very popular *Talking Labels* programme for its 130th anniversary, where people can visit the MyHeinz website and order bottles with custom-printed labels. [13] [14]

12 A limited edition Heinz ketchup bottle, distributed in The Netherlands, 2012

13 Heinz ketchup bottle from the *Talking Labels* programme, 2002

14 Plastic Heinz ketchup bottle from the *Talking Labels* programme, 1999

15 Technical drawing of the design of the Heinz bottle, 1960

NEXT PAGE:

16 Heinz '57 varieties' advertising, 1950s

90

12

13

14

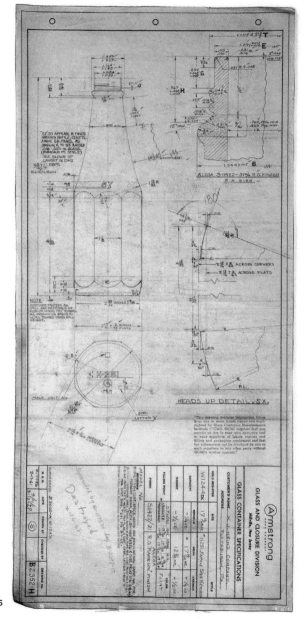

91

15

16

QUALITY STREET

SINCE 1836

More than 75 years ago the Mackintosh family had a flourishing toffee business in Halifax in the UK. In 1936, they decided to make chocolate available to the poor: they coated their toffees with chocolate, boxed them in brightly coloured tins and thus created the first chocolates to be sold at a moderate price. They named their new brand Quality Street after a play by J.M. Barrie (the author of *Peter Pan*); the name was also a pun on 'quality sweet' because normally only rich people could afford quality sweets as they contained exotic ingredients from around the world and were sold in elaborate packaging that cost as much as the contents.

From 1936 until 2000 Quality Street's visual brand identity was determined by the two characters featured on the box, both dressed in old-fashioned clothing: Major Quality and Miss Sweetly. [1] [6] [7] [8] [12] They were originally inspired by the principal characters of Barrie's *Quality Street* play, Phoebe Throssel and Valentine Brown, and were introduced as an answer to the people's craving for reminiscence. In the 1930s the UK was still burdened with the consequences of the economic crash; Mackintosh believed customers wanted to be reminded of a more stable, bygone era. Nostalgia was therefore an important element in the oldest designs of the Quality Street packaging. Nonetheless the brand was promoted with very modern marketing techniques. The company was a big advocate of advertising, which in those days was rather unusual for a confectionery business. They would frequently buy up the entire front page of national newspapers for their advertisements, which were beautifully detailed and illustrated in the style of the time.

1   Quality Street tin, 1940s

Quality Street was designed to be an entirely new, multi-sensory experience. The chocolates were packaged in a tin box instead of a cardboard one, so the scents would waft out as soon as it was opened. The different textures, colours, shapes and sizes of the sweets made opening the tin and consuming its contents a noisy, vibrant experience that the whole family could enjoy. It offered a moment of luxury for the common people. The different versions of the boxes over the years have always been beautifully decorated with illustrations of several romantic scenes starring Major Quality and Miss Sweetly, on the lid as well as all around the tin. The signature base colour varied from a warm red to a vibrant purple, but most of the time it was a bright magenta. [1][7][8][12] With every redesign, the illustration style also changed, while always remaining rather conventional and linked with the style of the time. Quality Street also has a rich history of marking Royal occasions (including Coronations, Royal Jubilees and marriages) with specially designed pieces of commemorative memorabilia.

The Quality Street logotype has evolved together with the illustrations and the overall design of the box, always matching the style of the time. For example, in the 1940s, the label featured a style of lettering with a delicate, connected script with almost the proportions and look of an upright italic. [1][2] This style of cursive is like an intermediate form between the roman and italic styles. Upright italics are characterized by letterforms with a cursive design at a very gentle or even absent slope angle. They sometimes provide the sole italic weight; at other times they act as a counterpart to the more common, cursive italic, providing a smart tool for typographic

2

Quality Street
3 CHOCOLATES & TOFFEES

Quality Street
4

**Quality
Street**
5

2 Quality Street logotype, 1940s
3 Quality Street logotype, 1950s
4 Quality Street logotype, 1970s
5 Quality Street logotype, 1990s
6 Quality Street tin, 1950s
7 Quality Street tin, 1950s
8 Quality Street tin, 1970s

6

7

8

articulation. A later example shows elegant lettering in a 1950s style, with a distinct handwritten feel to it. [3] [6] [7]

From approximately 1965 until the 1990s, Quality Street is designed with lettering in Didone style. [4] [8] This category of typeface is characterised by straight hairline serifs, a vertical orientation of the weight axes and high contrast between the thick and thin parts. Examples include the Bodoni, Didot and Walbaum typefaces. The style emerged in the late 18th century and has a 'modern' appearance. The heavy weights of this type style are often used for poster design. The type style used in the Quality Street example puts a 1970s spin on the classic style. There is a lot of movement going on in the shapes of the letters, the stems flow out into serifs and the form of a, t, Q and r is consistent with how they were designed for other typefaces at that time. [9] [10]

In the 1990s, the lettering was replaced by a more modest sans serif design. The style leans towards a humanist sans serif typeface, a type that is more calligraphic in structure, often with higher stroke contrast than other sans serifs. They have open forms that lead the eye horizontally, making them the best sans serifs for reading long texts and text in small type sizes. For the Quality Street logotype, some of the letters are treated with special features to make the type more appealing as a whole. For example, the Q is embellished with a long swash tail and the t and the y are drawn as a ligature to form a more coherent shape. [5] [12]
Today Quality Street sweets are sold in rectangular cardboard boxes and traditional tins and jars that still use the same logotype on a purple background. Nestlé acquired Rowntree Mackintosh and thus Quality Street in 1988 and has since then been able to maintain the strong brand image: according to Nestlé, 15 million tins of Quality Street were sold in 2010, enough sweets to stretch to the moon and back when placed end to end.

98

9 **Quality**

Quality

Quality

Quality

Quality

10

11

9 Part of the 1970s Quality Street logotype

10 Examples of Bauer Bodoni, Poster Bodoni, Didot and Walbaum

11 Current Quality Street logotype

12 Quality Street tin, 1990s

LA VACHE QUI RIT

SINCE 1898

The story of the legendary laughing cow starts back in 1921 in the Jura region in France, where founder Léon Bel thought of a new way of eating cheese and became the first to sell cheese packaged in individual portions. He set up a factory and automated the production process as much as possible. To keep the cheese fresh for longer, he used a wrapping technology, which, along with the iconic red tab for opening, was revolutionary at that time. How it exactly works is still a well-kept secret today.

Léon Bel trademarked his brand in France in 1921; the patent was the very first branded cheese product registered in France. By that time he had also already sketched the image of the cow that would become inextricably linked with his cheese. He had first seen it a few years earlier while he had been serving as a soldier for the French army during WWI; it had been painted on the trucks transporting the soldiers' meat rations. Alongside the figure of the cow was the word 'Wachkyrie', supposedly written to poke fun at the Germans' own supply trucks that were decorated with the mythical Walkyries of Norse legend. In French Wachkyrie is pronounced like *Vache qui rit* ('laughing cow') – and voila, Bel had a name for his product. In Bel's original drawing however, the cow wasn't laughing, it wasn't red and it wasn't wearing earrings. [1] Those elements are the work of Benjamin Rabier, a famous illustrator and personal friend of Bel, who edited the drawing in 1924 and modified it into something more like the image we know today. [3]

Bel not only had innovative ideas about his product, but also about marketing and advertising. In 1926, at a time when advertising was still

1 The first La Vache qui rit packaging with the illustration by Léon Bel, 1921

2 La Vache qui rit packaging, 1930s

3 Poster design by Benjamin Rabier, 1924

4 The current laughing cow

1

2

3

4

in its infancy, he had already established an internal advertising studio in his company. He displayed in dairy shops enamel signs and small statues depicting the laughing red cow. He even launched a series of products that customers could use at home, such as clocks, glassware and school supplies. In all of these advertising aids, in every poster and also on the packaging, the portrait of the red cow is the most prominent feature: it is not just a cow, but a personalized cow with human characteristics such as earrings and a smile that conveys enthusiasm. She has become a real icon, and is by far the most important element for recognising La Vache qui rit. This is all the more important as the brand name has been translated into different languages as the product conquered the international market: *The laughing cow, Den leende ko, A vaca que ri* and many others.

The typography on the posters and packaging takes a subordinate role, since it alone does not need to convey the brand's values and history; that is the role of the cow. When in 1924 Rabier designed the poster where the cow was depicted laughing for the first time, he painted the type of the brand name and information in an undecorated narrow sans serif style, which was often used by lettering artists at the time. [3] A later example of packaging, from the 1930s, shows beautiful bespoke Art Deco lettering. [2] The interesting details make this an outstanding example of fine craftsmanship, like the triangular crossbars of the E and the A, as well as the quirky curve of the C and the stylistic alternate version of the final S in the word *'fromageries'*.

　　The blue and white stripes around the box date from 1955. The cow's earrings, the position of which was altered in 1976 to show the top and the side,

depict the entire cheese box, using a Droste effect. Named after a Dutch cocoa brand, this effect is when a picture contains a smaller version of itself. The appearance is recursive: the smaller version contains an even smaller version of the picture, and so on. (The term for this effect in fine arts is *mise en abyme*.) [6]

The current La Vache qui rit box shows an open, friendly type that fits the brand image perfectly. [5] The words 'La Vache' are designed in a more cursive style, while the letterforms of 'qui rit' lean more towards those of an easy-going contemporary sans serif text face. The heavy smooth outstrokes on the a, V, c, etc. reflect the action of smearing La Vache qui rit cheese onto a slice of bread.

5

5　The current La Vache qui rit logotype
6　The current packaging of La Vache qui rit light

ST.RAPHAËL

SINCE 1900

104

The story of St.Raphaël begins in France in 1830. A certain Doctor Juppet worked night after night to develop an elixir based on quinine, a natural alkaloid with anti-inflammatory qualities and a typically bitter taste. However, his sight was deteriorating and so Juppet turned to archangel Raphaël, the patron saint of the blind. His prayers were answered and with his regained sight the doctor went on to create the perfect recipe for his liquor. St.Raphaël was born.

During the first few decades, the advertisements and packaging for St.Raphaël featured a rather typical graphic design, consistent with the graphic style of the times. Some posters from around 1900 and 1910 feature the archangel that supposedly led to the invention of the drink. [1] Later the archangel was replaced by two waiters, who have remained St.Raphaël's icons ever since. Representing the Ambré and Rouge versions of the aperitif, the waiters make a connection between the brand and the world of bistros (who better to advise you on your aperitif than a waiter in a chic French bistro) as well as French etiquette. [3][4]

The waiters acquired some extra flair in 1937, thanks to the French graphic artist Charles Loupot (1892–1962). He was asked by his friend Max Augier, the head of publicity for St.Raphaël, to rethink the brand's image because the company had just gained exclusive advertisement rights for the *Exposition Internationale des Arts et Techniques*.

    Loupot decided to base his 1937 redesign on the image of the two waiters, which was widely known and recognised; his main change at this stage was to add some movement to the two silhouettes, giving them a more dynamic feel. [8] It wasn't until after WWII that he redrew the

1 An early St.Raphaël advertisement, featuring an angel, 1910

2 The first use of two silhouettes and the signature colours (red, black and white) in a print advertising, 1932

3 Print advertising, France, 1935

4 Print advertising, France, 1936

1

LE S^T-RAPHAËL

QUINQUINA

Est le rafraîchissant sans égal, qui prévient
ou répare la fatigue...

2

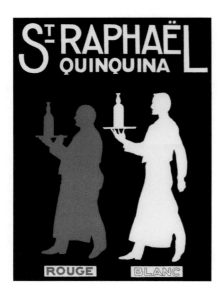

3

4

lettering. Up until then, St.Raphaël hadn't had a logotype, resulting in a variety of typestyles, from hand-drawn quirky lettering [5] to more modern letterforms. [2] [3] An example from 1935 even shows the use of both styles in one advertisement. [4] About 10 years later, Loupot replaced the former all-capitals lettering with a dynamic script; this change followed in the tradition of great French typographers like Roger Excoffon, the designer of typefaces with an unmistakably French identity, such as Mistral and Banco. [8] [10] The lettering has a loose and hand-drawn feel, as well as a constructed look. It looks like a precise balance between writing and drawing the letters with a broad-tip felt marker. Loupot created the lettering with an eye for precision and perfection, paying close attention to the proportions, the right angles and harmonious curves. [9] [10]

Loupot's work for St.Raphaël is one of the reasons why he became known as a specialist in poster design. He would keep on designing the St.Raphäel ads for the next 20 years. It's a pity that Loupot's iconic type, which was firmly rooted in the French graphic design tradition, no longer adorns the St. Raphaël image. Instead, early in the 21st century a new logotype was drawn that was only loosely based on the previous one; this is the one still used today. [7] Another change came in 2008, when one of the waiters was dropped and the remaining one got a new and more modern look.

The fact that Charles Loupot's work is still highly appreciated is reflected in a 1997 project by designer and illustrator Laurie Rosenwald and type designer Cyrus Highsmith. They developed a typeface based on Loupot's St.Raphaël logo; the result was

5

7

6

5 Print advertisement, 1905
6 Print advertisement, 1936
7 The current St.Raphaël logotype
8 Advertisement showing the redrawn waiters, 1953
9 Advertisement showing the new logo by Charles Loupot, 1952
10 Sketch and regulations for the logotype, 1947
11 Sketch for the image of the two waiters, 1947

quinquina

quinquina

8

9

10

11

quinquina

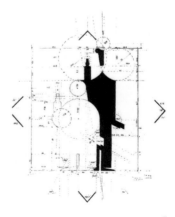

a fine script typeface, featuring the same qualities as the original letterforms, both calligraphic and industrial in style. It is important to state that while the designers were inspired by Loupot's work, they did not simply fill in the missing characters. [13] Important distinctions are for example the l, which Loupot drew with a loop on top, probably to give the logo enough weight on the right hand side. In the typeface, however, the l is treated like all the other letters with ascenders. The typeface is a connected script, which remains very legible in all-capital typesetting. The typeface, released by FontBureau in 1998, is rightly called 'Loupot'.

ST.RAPHAËL

s*Raphaël

St.Raphaël

12

12 Above: Banco by Roger Excoffon, 1951; middle: St-Raphaël lettering by Charles Loupot, 1938; below: Loupot typeface by Laurie Rosenwald and Cyrus Highsmith, 1997

13 Type specimens showing the Loupot typeface

NEXT PAGE:

14 Enamel advertising sign, 40 x 60 cm, 1958

APÉRITIF FRANÇAIS

rouge ambré-doré

CHARLES LOUPOT (1892–1962)

Laurie Rosenwald & Cyrus Highsmith

St.Raphaël

CALLIGRAPHIC AND INDUSTRIAL LETTERFORMS

ST.RAPHAËL QUINQUINA

McDONALD'S

When you look at McDonald's understated typographical first logo from 1940, [2] it is hard to believe it is a design for the same brand that is now one of the most recognisable icons in popular culture worldwide. The brothers Richard and Maurice McDonald opened a small, ordinary drive-in restaurant in California more than 70 years ago, unaware that a revolution in the food industry was to follow. Today, with more than 33,000 restaurants in 118 countries and serving more than 26 million customers a day, McDonald's dominates the fast food sector.

The company set up its first counter service for selling pre-made hamburgers, French fries and milkshakes in the early 1950s; they called it the Speedee Service System. This inspired one of the earliest versions of the McDonald's logo, from 1953, which featured a Speedee cartoon figure with a hamburger-shaped face. [3]

But it wasn't until 1954 that McDonald's became a brand, thanks to Ray Kroc. This milkshake machine salesman helped the McDonald brothers to extend their franchise concept by launching replicas of the original restaurant: a red and white tile building with its distinctive architectural features, namely two golden arches, one on each side of the building, bearing a slanted roof. These restaurants stood out and were prominent landmarks on the American roadside landscape for over two decades. Interestingly enough, when designing the first restaurant, architect Stanley Meston rejected Richard McDonald's idea of the golden arches; sign-maker George Dexter was hired to construct them later.

In 1961, Kroc became the sole owner of McDonald's and immediately set out his brand vision: 'a simple but effective consumer-driven premise of

1 McDonald's logo at a restaurant in Finland, 2013

2 The first McDonald's logo, 1940

3 McDonald's logo with the Speedee mascotte, 1953

4 McDonald's logo by Jim Schindler, 1962

5 McDonald's logo with the iconic M, 1985

1

2

3

4

5

quality, service, cleanliness, and value'. He was also a strong believer in marketing and advertising and decided to upgrade the company's image in 1962 with, among other things, a new logo. It was created by Jim Schindler, the company's head of engineering and design, who chose one very clear source of inspiration: the construction of the restaurants with the two golden arches. The symbol that was derived from them comprised two overlapping yellow bows, with a diagonal line cutting across them to symbolise the sloped roof. [4] As logo expert Andy Payne, creative director of Interbrand, has remarked, it is interesting that the McDonald's logo was born out of architecture, with the arches originally a design for a building but ending up creating the unique nature of the McDonald's M. Around the same time that the new logo was created, the company also introduced a mascot, the now legendary red-haired clown Ronald McDonald.

Seven years later the Golden Arches symbol was stylized into a more legible M. [5] [7] The arches are lighter at the top and the stems thicken towards the bottom. The design of the type of the McDonald's brand name is based on a Grotesque sans serif typeface, a style that includes Helvetica and Akzidenz Grotesque. [5] The letterforms of the Grotesques are monotone in weight, there is little stroke modulation and the stems are typically horizontal or vertical in direction. The aim of these sans-serif designs was to create a neutral typeface that had great clarity and no intrinsic meaning in its shape, so that it could be used on a wide variety of signage. This objective was met as many famous brands now use Helvetica for their iconic logotypes, including BMW, Evian, Nestlé and 3M. Although the McDonald's logotype shares

some design features with the Grotesque typefaces, its letterforms are custom-designed. Indications of this can be seen in the angled legs of M, the very short ascenders, the dark area at the connection of the stem and the shoulder of n and the apostrophe that has a different shape than the customary one. [8]

Today, the golden arched M is one of the most recognisable symbols in the western world. The term 'Golden Arches' is also used as a metonym, symbolizing capitalism or globalisation, since McDonald's is a prominent American corporation that has strived for international expansion. In line with its never-ending quest to stay in the hearts and minds of consumers worldwide, the company started a rebranding programme in 2006, including a drastic change of the look of its restaurants to make them more inviting places.

6 A McDonald's restaurant in England, 2013

7 The golden arched M

8 Above: the McDonald's letterforms; middle: the McDonald's brand name typeset in Helvetica Heavy; below: the McDonald's brand name typeset in Akzidenz Grotesk Black

6

7

8

McDonald's
McDonald's
McDonald's

PEPSI

SINCE 1898

116

The soda fountains that could be found at pharmacies in the 1800s were the local hangouts where villagers used to gather and talk about everything and anything. At a drugstore in New Bern, North Carolina, in 1898, the hot topic of conversation around its soda fountain was a new drink concocted by its pharmacist Caleb Bradham; the drink not only had digestive and refreshing benefits, but it also tasted good. Brad's Drink, as the creation was first called, was renamed Pepsi Cola in 1903. The origin of the name 'Pepsi' is debatable, but it is believed to be associated with the enzyme pepsin, which helps the digestive process. Bradham soon realised that he would reach more people by bottling his soda. This was the beginning of a success story that managed to endure, despite a few bumps along the way.

Pepsi's biggest competitor is of course Coca-Cola. The two brands have a long history of competition, with the term 'Cola Wars' used to describe the aggressive marketing campaigns from both PepsiCo – the company that owns Pepsi Cola – and the Coca-Cola Company. They each came up with a very distinct marketing strategy: Coca-Cola focused on celebrating holidays and nostalgia for childhood with advertising that had a family-friendly feel, while Pepsi chose to show celebrities recommending their products. Other marketing stunts were Pepsi's blind taste test, where the taste of Pepsi was chosen over Coca-Cola, and Pepsi Stuff, where people could collect points and redeem them for Pepsi lifestyle merchandising. (Read more about Coca-Cola's advertising on pp 82-86.)

Whereas Coca-Cola has a very recognizable and consistent design, Pepsi executed a series of redesigns for its logotype and packaging. The earliest version of the Pepsi logo was created in 1898 by Bradham's neighbour,

1

1 Pepsi bottle crowns, 1940s
2 Joan Crawford drinking Pepsi cola at the launch of Pepsi in Italy, 1960

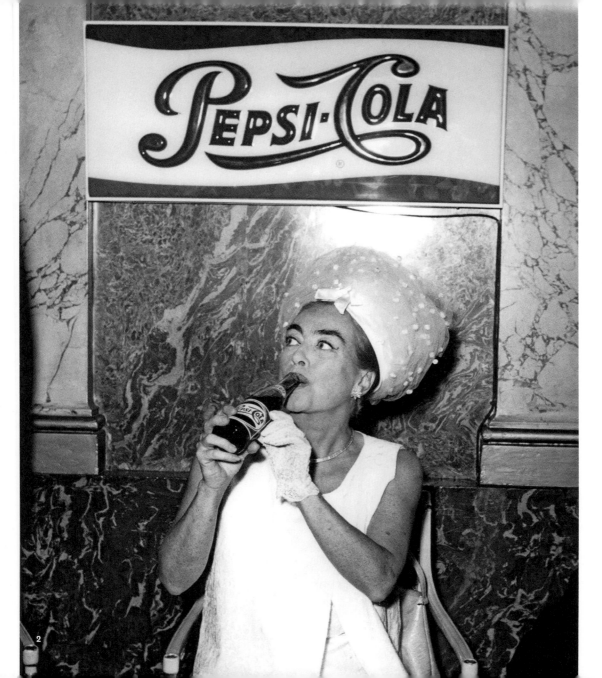

who was an artist. This is noticeable in the design: the letterforms are decorative but they also look rather naive and sketched. There is no consistency in stroke thickness or letter proportions. The design appears more like an illustration than a typographic logo. [3] In 1905, the letterforms were redrawn. Based on the same concept, the letters were given a cleaner look and more weight. The thorn-like serifs were shortened, while the long swashes were kept. [4] Just one year later, the Pepsi type got another make-over. The letters were now heavier and looked better constructed, while the serifs and stroke endings were redrawn in Tuscan style, a popular type style in that era (see the Maille text, pp 72-75). [5]

It was not until 1940 that the logo had a more radical redesign. The outlines of the letters were streamlined and the branched serifs were dropped. The new letterforms were based on a narrow bold sans serif, but are still hand-drawn or custom-designed. This is shown in the unstable base of the second P, the chunky lower half of S, the short leg on L and the top-heavy A. The swashes on P and C are refined and the loops in the curls replaced by heavy ball terminals. [6] In the 1940s, a new bottle design was also submitted, featuring a crown with the Pepsi logo. The signature colours were introduced at this time too, with the red, white and blue referring to the colours of the American flag, a nod of support to the war effort. Over the next two decades, the bottle cap would become the logo itself. [1] This is where the globe, which would later become a very important and recognizable image for the Pepsi brand, finds its origin.

3

4

5

6

3 The very first Pepsi logotype, 1898
4 Pepsi logotype, 1905
5 Pepsi logotype, 1906
6 Pepsi logotype, 1940
7 Pepsi drinking glass, 1961
8 Pepsi logotype, 1987
9 Pepsi logotype, 2008
10 Pepsi can, 2014

NEXT PAGE:

11 Landmark Pepsi Cola sign in NYC, 2013. This historic sign adorned once the Pepsi Factory and is now located at Gantry Plaza State Park.

7

8

9

10

In 1960, the Pepsi Cola brand name was shortened to Pepsi and the type of the logo got a rigorous makeover. The dynamic script was replaced by a neutral bold sans serif with wide letterforms. [7] With this evolution, Pepsi moved away from the Coca-Cola logo once and for all. In 1987, the letters were reshaped again, this time into typical 1980s letterforms, which were based on a geometric grid with straight horizontal curves. [8] In the new millennium, Pepsi chose a 3D approach in their visuals. The symbol of the globe was shadowed as were the letters, which also gained pointed sharp serifs.

By changing its logo so many times, the Pepsi brand has been able to keep its image up-to-date and in line with the trends and tastes of the time. So many changes, however, make it hard to keep a strong signature style. Pepsi consumers, unlike Coca-Cola drinkers or Starbucks lovers, were very accepting of change and for a long time seemed to go with the flow. However, when Pepsi redesigned its logo for the 16th time, in 2008, some unhappy fans spoke out. They didn't like the 'smiling' globe and felt the brand had strayed too far from its visual identity. [9][10] As for the changes to the letters, the heavy capitals of the Pepsi logo had been replaced with lighter lowercase letters, and the curved bar of the e now showed the movement of the signature wave that used to be part of Pepsi's globe symbol. The s however doesn't seem to blend in with the rest of design (it doesn't show the same features as the p and the e) and could have been drawn much wider, with more royal curves. [9]

Even since then, the Pepsi logo has undergone another gentle redesign, with changes introduced in 2012. The logo itself didn't change that much – the red, white and red blue are still very recognizable, making it easier for fans to identify with their brand this time than in 2008 – but it now appears in different ways and in different contexts. [10] It's all about creating new visual effects and about fitting the logo into the striking redesign of the bottle. Another example of an important element in the rebranding strategy, carried out by international design guru Mauro Porcini, is the launch of a premium glass bottle with a silver edge around the logo; with this bottle, Pepsi aims to reposition itself as a brand that is also available in more high-end establishments.

11

HEINEKEN

SINCE 1873

122

The Heineken success story began in 1864 when the 22-year-old Gerard Adriaan Heineken bought an Amsterdam brewery. Almost a decade later, in 1873, he renamed it *Heinekens Bierbrouwerij Maatschappij N.V.* and the family business brewed the first barrel of Heineken Lager. Gerard Heineken's product was an innovative one. He switched from traditional top to bottom fermentation and thereby created a new type of beermaking. Later he started using the A-yeast developed in 1886 by Doctor Elion, a student of Louis Pasteur; it is this yeast that gives the beer its characteristic flavour and is still today used exclusively by Heineken.

After World War I, the company began to focus more on exports. For example, after the alcohol prohibition in the United States ended in 1933, Heineken sent over a ship full of barrels of beer as a gift for the Americans who had had to wait more than 14 years for a drink. This proved to be a very smart marketing tactic because ever since then Heineken has been the most successful imported beer brand in the United States.

Smart marketing moves like this became a common occurrence when Alfred Heineken (nicknamed Freddy) expanded the brewery in the 1950s. He was a great believer in the power of advertising and marketing; in fact he was almost as much an advertising man as he was a brewer. Under his management an effective global strategy for the brand was established and he was very much involved in the development of Heineken's visual identity, which is built around the label on its beer bottle. This paper label in the shape of a racecourse (a rectangle with rounded corners) [1][2] contains several interesting typographic elements. The most prominent part is the black band with the Heineken logotype, in the centre of the label. Other textual information is typeset in neutral and straightforward

1

1 A Heineken label, 1964

2 The current Heineken label

condensed sans serif capitals and arranged along the borders of the label. The letterforms of the Heineken logotype reflect a historic style in their shape and style. The style is a robust seriffed type, but also shows an unexpected elegant feature in the outstroke of the n, a characteristic that is more likely to be seen in cursive type styles. The H and the k show very short ascenders, a space-saving feature that makes these letterforms look like they are from a heavy-duty text typeface. The heavy wedged serifs have the connotation of keeping 'both feet firmly on the ground', reflecting in this case an uncomplicated business approach. This is a good example of the underlying message that type can tell. The whole label breathes Heineken's heritage and authenticity. [2]

According to company folklore, the Heineken letterforms were originally drawn with horizontal bars in the middle of the 3 e's. However, this made the logotype appear too formal for a beer label, so, when Freddy was in charge, the e's were tilted backwards and became what Heineken calls 'the smiling e'. [4] Maybe unknowingly, this feature links the Heineken type with one of Holland's archetypal examples in type design, the Hollandse Mediæval by S.H. De Roos. De Roos designed this new typeface in 1912, becoming the first Dutchman to achieve such an accomplishment in 150 years. This typeface was the first modern Dutch printing type and was used for several decades. [5]

124

Als papa deze af heeft,
moet-ie even rusten.

3

Heineken®
4

Chevalets de lecture
Installations d'usines

5

3   Heineken advertisement from
    The Netherlands, 1988

4   The letterforms of the Heineken
    logotype

5   Example of the typeface Hollandse
    Mediæval, with the e's with a
    diagonal bar, by S.H. De Roos, 1912

6   Heineken beer bottle, 2013

Heineken uses a second logo too: the Heineken star, also called the authenticity logo. This red star with its strong symbolic value communicates and reinforces the modernity, originality and vitality of the brand. It's an important branding element that's applied in different kinds of communication, merchandise and packaging. [3] It also appears on the labels of the newly redesigned green beer bottles. The green colour itself, however, isn't new at all: it has been a distinctive feature of the brand ever since Heineken reached American shores in 1933, packed in squat green bottles. After WWII the green colour became associated with high-quality beer because it was typically used by European brewers, who were known to produce beer of a much higher quality than the Americans, or at least they priced their beers that way. The actual reason why they used green glass was a practical one: there was a shortage of brown glass after the war. Nonetheless, green bottles became a status symbol. Realising how important the appearance of the bottle was to create a lasting impression, Freddy Heineken stuck with the green colour and it has been a permanent feature of the Heineken brand ever since.

Freddy also claimed that he came up with one of the best known Heineken slogans 'Heerlijk, helder, Heineken' ('Delicious, clear, Heineken'), which works well because of the alliteration in Dutch. Other sources however claim that the tagline was written by the Dutch poet and copywriter Martin Veltman and Peter Knegjens, a sports commentator and advertising man. Be that as it may, the tagline has proven to be a good one and was used until 1990. In more recent years Heineken has been working with different agencies for specific campaigns. For example Dutch advertising company TWBA\Neboko came up with slogans for Heineken like 'Biertje?' (Beer?) and in 2007 'Serving the planet'. In 2011 the 'Open your world' tagline was introduced for marketing across the globe to convey the brand's worldly, open-minded and confident personality.

VAN NELLE

SINCE 1837

In 1782 Johannes van Nelle and his wife Hendrica opened a small shop in Rotterdam where they sold coffee, tea and tobacco. A few decades later, in 1837, the Van der Leeuw family took a stake in the firm and business started to flourish. Jacobus Johannes van der Leeuw established global trade contacts, founded Van Nelle's own plantations in the Dutch East Indies and transformed what was once a small shop into a factory for roasting coffee and processing tobacco and tea. Around the turn of the century, the consumption of tea and coffee was on the rise and the Van Nelle business prospered.

The Van Nelle company distinguished itself with a distinctive marketing approach, for example by publishing from 1920 onwards a series of children's books about a gnome called Piggelmee. The first story *Piggelmee en het tovervisje* ('Piggelmee and the magic fish') was based on a fairy tale by the Brothers Grimm and adapted to promote Van Nelle coffee – after all the books were first and foremost a form of advertising for the company. Piggelmee became very popular and holds a place in the collective memory of the Dutch. Nowadays, long after his disappearance, old books, records and other Piggelmee products have become popular collector's items. [1]

The distinctive branding approach of Van Nelle in the 1920s and 1930s, when the company was run by Kees van der Leeuw, not only speaks from their smart use of the Piggelmee character but also from the look of the advertisements and the packaging of the products (coffee, tea and cigarettes). This look was created by graphic and type designer Jac. (Jacob) Jongert (1883–1942), who was hired by Van der Leeuw in 1920. Jongert not only had a fine feeling for art but also for commerce. He was an

1

1 Pin with the image of Piggelmee, 1960s
2 The iconic Van Nelle coffee and tea box, designed by Jac. Jongert, 1933

advocate of collaboration between artists/designers and businessmen, believing that art could serve and lift up business. Influenced by the wishes of the commercial environment, his artwork for Van Nelle is characterized by a certain simplicity and a functional approach; his letters and colours are powerful and his shapes angular, but nevertheless his designs have an ornamental character. Although he was passionate about the design principles of the Avant-Garde, Jongert's advertising and packaging designs reflect diverse modern influences. For example, the use of the primary colours yellow, red and blue as well as the strong contrasts reference constructivist design principles. His yellow-red coffee/tea box, which is featured in the MoMA in New York, is without a doubt his best-known piece of design. [2]

As for the letterforms, Jongert insisted on drawing them all by hand. It shows his exquisite designing skills and it also allowed him to modify the height and width of the letters so that he had a flexible lettering system. Jongert's typographical designs show hand-drawn, straightforward sans serif capital letters with a constructed look and that vary in width. Instead of disturbing the typographic rhythm of the words, the extended and condensed letterforms make the lettering look like a piece of fine, bespoke craftsmanship. [3] It is not unusual that it is a sans serif style that inspired Jongert's signature lettering style. Sans serif was a novelty in typography at the beginning of the 19th century and was mainly used for titling and display purposes and advertising and poster typesetting. Sign painters and lettering artists adopted the style early on.

VAN
NELLE'S
!
TABAK

3 Van Nelle coffee packaging, designed
   by Jac. Jongert, 1935
4 Van Nelle tea packaging, 1955
5 Enamel advertising sign, designed by
   Jac. Jongert, 1932

4

5

Jongert had started working at Van Nelle as a packaging designer but quickly earned the title 'head of advertising'. He was given absolute freedom at Van Nelle: sales were high, and his designs and decisions went unquestioned. The corporate identity he designed for the company became a milestone in the Dutch design world. His commercial attitude and strong business sense meant that Jongert had become well known and celebrated, not only as a designer but also as one of the first publicity agents in the Netherlands. Until then, the image of a company had not been created by advertising agencies – they simply didn't exist – but by painters and illustrators who created the packaging and advertisements.

The strong brand image that he created for Van Nelle was underlined by the factory building that was constructed between 1927 and 1929. [7] It was commissioned by director Kees Van der Leeuw, a smart business-man and also a philanthropist with a fine and modern taste in art and architecture. Van der Leeuw hired architect Leendert van der Vlugt, who designed a marvellous modern factory that would become the epitome of the new architecture style *Nieuwe Bouwen* in the Netherlands, characterized by functionality, geometry and a lack of architectural decoration. The factory also shows influences of Russian constructivism, visible in the large sign letters on the roof of the building. [9] The Van Nelle factory is an important landmark in Rotterdam and is recognized as a Dutch national monument. It currently houses new media and design companies. [8]

After Jongert's death in 1942, Van Nelle continued along the same path with its advertising: straightforward packaging designs with sans serif capital lettering. [4] The latest example of a Van Nelle product (the company closed in 1995), dating back to the mid-1980s, is a storage box for rolling tobacco. The logo is formed out of heavy, condensed sans serif letterforms, with clear modernist roots.

6

6 Jongert also drew an uppercase alphabet in the same style as Van Nelle's constructed geometrical letters, but the letterforms work better as the flexible lettering system than in the form of a static alphabet on paper.

7 Van Nelle factory, Rotterdam, 1930

8 Van Nelle design factory, Rotterdam, 2013

9 Van Nelle architectural type

7 FABRIEK VAN NELLE TE ROTTERDAM   ARCH IR J BRINKMAN EN L vd VLUGT
USINES DE VAN NELLE À ROTTERDAM

8

9

LA BALEINE

SINCE 1934

La Baleine is a brand of salt, but not just any salt: it's naturally evaporated sea salt from the Mediterranean Sea, available in coarse crystals (*gros*) and as a fine grain (*fin*). For most of its lifetime, La Baleine salts have been mined exclusively in the Aigues-Mortes saltworks in the Camargue region in France. Recently, however, grey sea salt from the Atlantic Ocean has been added to the mix.

The brand was introduced to the French market in 1934, and from the very beginning La Baleine has been represented by the image of a whale. It was inspired by a character in the book *Gédéon traverse l'Atlantique* by the famous French illustrator Benjamin Rabier, who also created the image of the cow for the cheese brand La Vache qui rit (see p. 100). La Baleine's whale survived several packaging redesigns and is still the icon used today. Nonetheless its appearance has been updated several times over the past 80 years, keeping in style with the times with every redesign. [1]

In 1934 the whale icon started out as an illustrated, cartoon-like character, with its tail in the air and a spouting fountain. [2] Next to it on the packaging was a bold Art Deco display typeface. In the next decade, this typeface was replaced by a strong and sturdy slab serif type with heavy block serifs, together with a sans serif version of the same typeface. [3] In 1955, the illustration of the whale became more dynamic. [4] At the same time, the logo was also modified slightly, a strategy that we will see time and again over the next decades. Every time the packaging is altered, the whale and the logo are both adjusted to reflect those changes. The typographic design of the 1955 box shows a variety of typefaces, the most prominent word and style naturally being '*sel*', the French word for salt. It is typeset in heavy condensed capital letters in Egyptienne style, a

1 Overview of the different versions of the La Baleine whales, 1934–2014
2 À La Baleine packaging, 1934
3 À La Baleine packaging, 1940s
4 Digitised À La Baleine logo from 1955, 2012
4 À La Baleine packaging, 1955

1

2

3

4

5

kind of slab serif type with long and heavy serifs. This utilitarian type style strongly contrasts with the script type of '*de Mer*' and '*grené seché*'. The design of this cheerful script style is based on brush-painted letters and is a classic example of mid-20th century French typography, in the style of the great French masters like Roger Excoffon (see the St.Raphaël text, pp 104-111). [5]

In 1960, the whale was completely redesigned in order to fit the rest of the packaging. [6] It was drawn in graphic outlines and became more of a logo and less of an illustration. The whale also faces to the right now. The type style of the packaging redesign in 1960 is an archetypical example of 1960s typography, where the main focus is on form. [7] The letters are all of an equal width and are horizontally and vertically aligned, at the expense of the design of the individual letterforms. The letters are probably hand drawn, based on the immensely popular Swiss neutral style of Helvetica. Here the S looks a bit unbalanced and the R is missing Helvetica's representative double curved leg.

When the brand's name changed from 'À La Baleine' to 'La Baleine' in 1970, the company also adopted a new logo and packaging [8]. The whale icon was transformed into an even more graphic version and took up less space on the packaging. The type at that time was set in a style similar to Poster Bodoni Bold Italic, a style that was very popular in the 1970s. Poster Bodoni was designed in 1929 by the American typesetter Chauncey H. Griffith; it was an addition for bold poster typesetting to the typefaces based on the work of Giambattista Bodoni, the well-known typographer, type designer and ducal printer in Parma in the late 18th and early 19th centuries. The Bodoni styles are characterized by an extreme contrast

6

7

8

9

between thick and thin strokes, an overall geometric construction and flat, unbracketed serifs. In the Italics, the typeface shows a very elegant style, with fine upward outstrokes on the letters [10].

The type and the whale symbol were combined into one logo in 1988, featuring a seriffed, geometrical typeface. [9] The current logo gained its final shape in 1993, when the whale symbol and type were redesigned to be more rooted in the original style of La Baleine's packaging. [11] The whale itself was revived in the style of the original illustration of 1934, with a very stylized pen drawing. 'La' is designed in a cursive style, with the strokes of L showing flowing lines, resembling the tail of a whale. The word 'Baleine' underneath is set in capital letters and drawn to form a harmonious entity together with the whale symbol. [12] [13]

11

12

13

sel de mer
sel de mer
sel de mer

10

6 À La Baleine packaging, 1960

7 À La Baleine logo, 1960s

8 La Baleine packaging, 1970s

9 La Baleine packaging, 1988

10 Above: Bodoni Bold; Middle: Poster Bodoni; Below: Poster Bodoni Italic

11 La Baleine packaging, 1993

12 La Baleine packaging, 2013

13 Logo for La Baleine's 80th anniversary, 2014

FURTHER READING

On the history of typography, graphic design and branding:

Steven Heller and Louise Fili, *Scripts – Elegant Lettering From Design's Golden Age*. Thames & Hudson, 2011.

David Jury, *Graphic Design before Graphic Designers — The Printer as Designer and Craftsman 1700 – 1914*. Thames & Hudson, 2012.

Marcel Verhaaf, *The Heinz ketchup bottle*. Bis Publishers, 2011.

Christophe Zagrodzki, *Charles Loupot*. Le cherche midi éditeur, 1998.

On logo and graphic design:

Ron Van der Vlugt, *Logo Life – Life histories of 100 Famous Logos*. Bis Publishers, 2012.

www.logodesignlove.com

www.behance.net

On marketing, branding and creative advertising:

www.creativebloq.com

www.brandchannel.com

THANK YOU

Many thanks to all those without whom this book would
never have been possible:

all the people working at the respective food brand companies who helped
    me by providing images and information;

Karoline Neujens, for starting this project with me and for writing the first
    drafts of the texts about the histories of the brands;

everyone at Luster Publishing for their patience during the making
    of this book. A special thanks to Karin De Bruyn for providing extra
    information about branding and the brand histories;

Anna Jenkinson and Hadewijch Ceulemans, for reworking the texts;

Tom Andries, for agreeing to write a foreword for this book;

Marcel Verhaaf and Paulien Hassink, for helping out with some of the
    images for the Heinz chapter;

the collectors and photographers whose images are printed in this book;

Roeland and Mil;

Tim and Jen;

Frie and Ellen.

JOKE GOSSÉ already focused on typography during her studies in graphic design at Sint Lucas Antwerp (2002-2006). In 2008 she obtained her MA in Typeface Design from the Department of Typography & Graphic Communication at the University of Reading (UK). Since then, Joke has been working as a type designer on several bespoke typefaces for cultural and editorial projects, as well as on self-initiated projects. She also works as a freelance graphic designer and typographer. She is the author and designer of *Attractive Things Work Better* (2012), a book with 50 typographically designed quotes and wisdoms.

PHOTO CREDITS

TASTY **STORIES**
LEGENDARY FOOD BRANDS AND THEIR TYPEFACES

Compilation, texts, photo editing, graphic design
  Joke Gossé

Text editing
  Anna Jenkinson

ISBN 978 94 6058 1014
NUR 802
D/2014/12.005/2

© 2014, Luster, Antwerp
www.lusterweb.com